NOT JUST TALKING

NOT JUST TALKING
Conversational Analysis, Harvey Sacks' Gift to Psychotherapy

*A New Model Showing How the Management of the Therapeutic
Dialogue is Vital for a Successful Outcome in Psychotherapy*

Jean Pain

KARNAC

First published in 2009 by
Karnac Books Ltd
118 Finchley Road
London NW3 5HT

British Library Cataloguing in Publication Data

A C.I.P. for this book is available from the British Library

ISBN-13: 978-1-85575-689-2

Typeset by Vikatan Publishing Solutions (p) Ltd., Chennai, India

Printed in Great Britain

www.karnacbooks.com

Also by Jean Pain

So You Think You Need Therapy
So You Want to be a Therapist

CONTENTS

ACKNOWLEDGEMENTS

My first acknowledgement has to be to Dr Ian Hutchby, now Professor of Sociology at Leicester University who supervised my PhD. Ian always read my work with great care. His high standards enabled me to think more clearly and to remain closely in touch with my main argument. I wish to thank Dr Charles Antaki, Professor of Linguistics and Social Psychology at Loughborough University who was my external examiner and appreciated my work.

I am grateful to David Silverman who was particularly helpful to me in two ways. He helped me to find my supervisor and his book on qualitative research made me aware of the changes that were taking place in research methodology.

For the last few years I have been teaching my findings to my daughter, Catherine Pain and her husband Dan Wait. Working by myself and making my own decisions has been my *modus vivendi*. I have not found it easy to break the habit of a lifetime. It is thanks to the extraordinary flexibility and qualities of mind of Kate and Dan that I have benefited by their comments on my writing. Bob Pain has given me unfailing support as always, especially with regard to the quality of my writing. Although we work in very different fields he has always been available to give me his point of view when I needed it.

Liz Ackroyd, the research administrator at Brunel was always ready to give me her time whilst I was working on my thesis. She was unfailingly cheerful and helpful in answering my numerous questions about general academic procedures.

Last but not least I greatly appreciate the generosity of those clients who agreed to let me make use of their own material. I learned as much from them as they learned from me.

PREFACE

My first and foremost interest is what makes people tick. From my earliest memories I have been fascinated by the way people talk to each other and the power we have to influence others with the spoken word. I have been an avid reader and observer all my life. With an outsize sensitivity and imagination, childhood and adolescence were difficult times for me, especially as I was growing up during the Second World War and becoming more and more horrified by what was going on in the outside world. Like many young people I was searching for answers.

Up at university reading Spanish, I shared a room with a girl studying social science. Always interested in other people's books, I came across Freud for the first time. I cannot remember which book it was, but I read it in a few days from cover to cover. I was mesmerised. Here at last was someone who presented me with some good arguments about human nature. My deep depression about the state of the world began to lift.

I knew that sooner or later I wanted to work as a psychotherapist. But first I needed to understand myself better and overcome my overwhelming emotional responses to other people's misery. As a natural rebel, I have always asked questions and sought answers from books rather than from people. As a child I preferred my own company. I found it difficult to make friends because I could not find anyone who shared my interests. From then on my preferred reading was in the realms of psychology and philosophy as well as the literature I had always loved.

However, I knew I needed other people. The problem was where to find them. My answer was to do what I wanted to do, to let nothing stand in my way, and to practice the gentle art of talking with others. Only then did I begin to find people I could talk with about the great questions of good and evil. Looking back over my life I am astounded by what I have achieved through facing my fears and taking risks. Not having been 'socialised' as a child, I had to find my own path to the realisation that there are no perfect relationships and, consequently, that all relationships involve conflict but some are much better than others.

I realised it was a huge advantage not to have been socialised at school, nor at home. I learned to do it in my own way and I surprised myself when, once I got going, I awakened within me a talkative and sociable being that I never knew existed. I was over fifty when I finally trained as a therapist, and into my sixties when I returned to academic studies to understand what I was doing with my clients that produced good results.

As a psychotherapist in private practice I was interested into the links between the therapeutic dialogue and the process of psychotherapy. Through comparing everyday conversation with the therapist/client dialogue I was able to isolate similarities and differences.

The culmination of my life's work was the award of my PhD at Brunel University in 2003. My research enabled me to find answers to two questions that had long puzzled me. First, how does the dialogue, under the guidance of therapists and the reactions and responses of clients make it possible for them to make beneficial changes in the way they manage their lives? Second, how is it that many of us find it so difficult to maintain relationships, especially close ones?

I have spent two years putting the new ideas I developed into a form that lay people as well as specialists can understand. Inevitably I have had to use some technical language. There is a glossary in the appendices that will help. The first time I use a word that belongs to my particular methodology, conversation analysis, it is printed in bold, so that readers know they cannot be expected to understand it and can look it up in the glossary.

INTRODUCTION

The springboard for my PhD was the work of Harvey Sacks. His method is called **conversation analysis** (henceforward referred to as CA). He was a towering genius who was ahead of his time. A polymath, he first took his BA at Columbia, then was awarded a scholarship to study law at Yale where he realised his real interest lay in how institutions, such as law, could work. He was not interested in practising law based on what he had been taught, but in exploring the possibilities for enhancing the process itself (Schegloff, in Sacks, 1992a, p. xii/iii). He was more interested in how activities were carried out in practice by real people in real situations rather than in the traditional rules on which activities were based.

With this purpose in mind he then went to Harvard to pursue this interest. There he met Harold Garfinkel, who was on a sabbatical leave from the University of California. Garfinkel was busy developing a branch of sociology called **ethnomethodology**, which constitutes the study of social behaviour. During this period Sacks met a kindred spirit, Emmanuel Schegloff, who was to play an important part in the development of CA and in editing the lecture notes when they were finally published. Sacks, acting on the advice of his law teacher, Laswell, decided to study sociology at Berkeley. He became one of the first graduate fellows of the newly established Center for the Study of Law and Society at that university, together with his friend Schegloff. He maintained his connection with Garfinkel, following his development of ethnomethodology closely.

In 1963, Garfinkel arranged for Sacks to be given an appointment as Acting Professor of Sociology at the University of California with the first year off. Sacks was to serve as a Fellow at the Center for the Scientific Study of Suicide in Los Angeles. The Centre was staffed by academics who, as part of their social science research, listened to telephone calls from people who felt suicidal. At the same time Schegloff's work brought him to Los Angeles in the summer of 1963, enabling the two friends to continue their friendship and their work relationship during that year.

The Center focused on 'psychological autopsies' based on the examination of psychiatric, and especially psychodynamic theorising (Schegloff, in Sacks, 1992a, p. xv). The data comprised audio recordings of the telephone calls. All Sacks' previous work had been a preparation for a new interest, the study of live conversation itself. Working within the context of psychotherapy as a social activity awakened Sacks' interest in psychotherapy. He went on to study group therapy sessions with young people. This was of great interest to Schegloff and Sacks. Psychodynamic theorising led them to a concern with dialogue and in particular with Platonic dialogue as a form of discourse designed to control conduct. Moreover Sacks' curiosity led to new readings. He studied Freud and Opie and Opie (1969), who were concerned with the effect of society on children's development, and he became interested in archaeology and biblical studies. Audio recordings of telephone calls made to the Center provided the data he needed to study the process of **talk-in-interaction**.

Sacks was awakened to the possibilities of researching the fascinating topic of what was actually going on in these telephone calls. For instance, how did the callers manage to manoeuvre their responses so that they could get away with not giving their names? It was the formulation of this question that aroused Sacks' awareness of the power of talk-in-interaction, giving him the first inkling of how talk as a topic could be studied in a systematic way and some underlying rules abstracted. "There is the distinctive and utterly critical recognition here the *talk can be examined as an object in its own right*, and not merely as a screen on which are projected other processes" (Schegloff, 1992a, p. xviii) (my emphasis).

Sacks had finally found his life's work. He had a huge task in front of him: to find out what it is that we do in conversation that we do not know we are doing. This was new ground. He set out to create a method that would enable him to find out the covert social rules of conducting conversation that enable us to engage in intelligible discourse. Sacks himself was all too well aware that this was not going to be easy.

One of my reasons for undertaking academic research is that as a practising psychotherapist I have often found myself in conflict with certain assumptions of my own professional training. My work was on the whole successful, in that most of my clients made changes in their lives, and I did not know how this happened. It was a consolation and an inspiration to me to read "We still hardly know what causes a behavioural change in a client and what factors are effective for such a change." (Siegfried, 1995, p. 1).

Whatever the training and techniques of any particular therapist, the vehicle for the process of psychotherapy is the dialogue itself, which, according to Siegfried (1995) offers a unique way of studying how psychotherapy works. A major problem for the understanding of psychotherapy is that it is a fragmented profession. There are over 400 different methods (Feltham & Horton, 2000, p. 693). This is very confusing for would-be therapists and would-be clients. How do they choose which path to follow? Sacks' unique approach to the understanding of dialogue offers the possibility of a unifying factor that could be applied to all kinds of 'talking therapy'.

I conducted my PhD research under the aegis of the social sciences. In this way I could treat psychotherapy as a social activity and focus on the particular way in which this particular activity affected the **talk-in-interaction**, and conversely how the structure of the dialogue itself defined the structure of the therapeutic process.

The findings of my PhD research reveal that talk in psychotherapy is based on everyday conversation, but differs from it in some significant ways. Effective psychotherapy is more likely when the relationship between therapist and client is founded on a basis of mutual respect. Whatever the professional training of psychotherapists, they need this skill to manage the therapeutic relationship.

If their expertise in cooperative conversation lags behind their professional knowledge the work is less likely to be successful.

Psychotherapy offers us the opportunity to understand ourselves: to acknowledge things about ourselves that we would rather sweep under the carpet. Through the research into clients' difficulties in talking about painful subjects, it became clear that therapists get results when they take great care in the way they structure their own side of the conversation and in the way they respond to clients. The data consists of audio recordings of live therapy sessions, which are then transcribed into documents with a special notation for paralinguistic elements, such as pauses, laughter and the lowering or raising of volume (see Appendix 2). There are no theories to be explored.

I discovered far more about the importance of dialogue than I could have hoped for. *I realised that the particular difficulties involved in helping clients to understand their problems in living could be greatly helped by changes in the way they use language, both to themselves and to others.*

Sacks' lecture notes comprise his thinking over a period of some ten years and abruptly came to an end when he was tragically killed in 1975 in a car accident. Because he was ahead of his time, few people recognised the importance of his work. He recognised that some of the problems that arise in conversation are the result of what we are trying to do with it: transform the complexity of our thoughts into meaningful sounds. The spoken language has enormous, unused potential.[2] He always had a small body of enthusiasts who believed in him and continued to develop his ideas. Fortunately, one of his most dedicated students, Gail Jefferson, ensured that his lectures were recorded and transcribed. Jefferson devised a special notation that took account of **paralinguistic phenomena**, such as silences and laughter. Appendix 1 comprises a list of this notation based on her work. Yet Sacks' notes were not published in book form and therefore not widely available until their publication, edited by Schegloff, in 1992. Thus the body of CA research is relatively small, although there has been an increasing recognition of the value of his work over the last two decades.

My research shed light on something that had puzzled me since I was a child. Why do we feel 'hurt' or 'upset' by apparently innocuous remarks? Why do we sometimes feel we 'do not know what to say'? Why is talk fraught with difficulties? In this book I hope to bring into focus that the way we conduct conversation, either with ourselves or with others can be an important element in the cause of many of our ills leading to the overwhelming popularity of counselling and psychotherapy today.

The organisation of the book

The book is divided into two parts of similar length:

PART I

The principles of speech and human social behaviour

PART II

The therapeutic dialogue in practice

The first part is a summary of the effect of social and psychological human behaviour on the way we talk with each other. The second part constitutes selected transcripts from spontaneous talk between me and my clients. These extracts demonstrate how my new model for the therapeutic dialogue works in practice. Both parts are complete in themselves. The first part provides background material that makes the second part more comprehensible, but the second part can stand on its own and be read first if the reader so desires.

The appendices include extended stretches of talk from which the extracts have been taken. Read separately, they give the reader a taste of the vitality and humour that comes to the surface in the therapeutic dialogue.

Conclusion

Throughout the book, there are two recurrent themes to which attention must be paid if the task of therapy is to be achieved. First, the need for ongoing adherence to **relevance, coherence** and **cooperation.** Whenever we are carrying out some kind of action through conversation, whether it is passing the time of day with a friend or problem solving in different contexts, such as business or psychotherapy, it is constant attention to these three sub-topics that enhances the possibility of a successful outcome. In any conversation, both parties need to tailor what they say to each other in order to ensure, as far as that is possible, that they bear in mind to whom they are talking. For instance, if we talk about 'John', without asking ourselves if the person we are talking to knows who you mean by 'John', this can cause confusion and lead to incoherence. The same applies to the writing of a book. The author needs to stick to the point, to write in an intelligible way, in order to gain the attention and cooperation of the reader.

Second, the recognition that clients alone have the key to their problems. Therapists guide them through showing them ways in which they can identify their problems. The cutting edge of psychotherapy research today is the culmination of the enormous changes in thinking during the course of the 20th century. Three of these changes have great importance for the understanding of how human beings can work to explore the possibilities to improve their quality of life and their communication with each other. They are:

• The shift away from the compartmentalisation of different disciplines and the recognition that such domains as philosophy, psychology and the social sciences can only be fully understood when we attend to the effect that each has on the others.
• The development and growth of psychotherapy practice.
• The change in the way we understand language and how we use it in conversation.

Some of these topics will be explored in the first chapter.

NOTES

1. Although all of us have the same fundamental needs, each of us seeks to satisfy them in our own unique way. Hence there is no one method for approaching any particular kind of problem. Moreover, our knowledge of how the mind works, and how people interact with themselves and with others, is still in a very primitive state. Hence learning to understand oneself is difficult enough, and if we cannot manage that how can we hope to understand another? However, the vast library of knowledge about human nature, as exemplified by great works of literature and psychological theory provides us with guidelines within which we can work. How we make use of this knowledge to look continually for clues to underlying personal patterns of behaviour is itself an art form. We can

never know whether we are working on the right lines except through how our clients respond to our work. This why the great figures in the understanding of human nature, for example the philosopher Wittgenstein and the psychoanalyst Wilfred Bion constantly stressed the importance of accepting one's own ignorance. I do not know but I am willing to try to find out. An open mind is the first prerequisite and one that Sacks possessed in abundance.
2. Sacks (1992a, p. 429) quoted Uriel Weinreich in Joseph Greenberg (ed.) Universals of Language (1963), pp. 117–118.

"In a remarkable passage, Sapir likens language to a dynamo capable of powering an elevator but ordinarily operating to feed an electric doorbell. Language is used more often than not in ways that do not draw upon its full semantic capacity. In its 'phatic' functions, when speech is used merely to signify the presence of a sympathetic interlocutor, it easily becomes 'desemanticised' to a formidable extent. In its various ceremonial functions, language may come to be desemanticised by still another mechanism... The more pressing task for linguistics, it seems to me, is to explain the elevator, not the doorbell; avoiding samples of excessively casual or ceremonial speech, to examine language under conditions of its fully-fledged utilisation."

PART I

The Principles of Speech and Human Social Behaviour

CHAPTER ONE

The silent revolution

The aim of this chapter is twofold. First I shall compare the ways in which language has been studied up to the nineteenth century and into the twentieth, with the new approach that sees language in a wider context, looking not only at structure but at how structure is indissolubly linked to function, meaning and the understanding of how the mind works.

Second, this movement has come into being in tandem with another revolution, the recognition that boundaries between different domains are not nearly as clear as earlier scientists believed. Korzybski's monumental work (1933) revealed the connections between many different disciplines. The most important one is implicated by the title of his work—*Semantics and Sanity*. In one stroke Korzybski opened our eyes to the realisation that how we use language reflects our mental processes and affects our mental and physical well-being.

Speech and grammar

No-one knows how the capacity for speech came into being. When our ancestors began to develop speech, no-one was there to teach them. The only way they could learn was by trial and error. Mistakes could only be identified pragmatically through failures in the transmission of meaning to another person. What worked was adopted, what failed to work was rejected. This rule-of-thumb criterion enabled them to build a structured system of verbal communication and assimilate it for future use. It continues to be useful to us in establishing communication through **talk-in-interaction**.

This process provided the basis for the analysis of the structure of a language that we call grammar. There are many different kinds of grammar. All are attempts to define structure. Cogswell & Gordon (1996) is a useful introduction to Chomsky's work.[1] He looked at the way people constructed sentences and discovered that there is an economy in their use of words that results in short cuts (see Chapter Three). He found that such economies exist in all languages and that all languages have much in common in their structure. This led him to develop his theory of universal grammar. He took one giant stride further by recognising the connection between the human mind and language. He realised that we did not learn the structure of words through imitation alone. We already possessed the innate ability to construct grammatical forms for ourselves. He named this aspect of the human brain the language faculty.

The search for the understanding of how conversation works

Structure and content are two separate things that are connected to each other through one important factor, their function.[2] Sacks was the first person to realise that we needed to look first at the purpose of conversation because purpose defines meaning. Once we know why we are talking together, what social purpose we aim to achieve, we can organise the structure under the guidance of the purpose. If structure and content do not fit we shall not achieve our purpose. Thus Sacks defined different kinds of talk as **speech-exchange systems** that only come into being as a result of the need to carry out an activity. For example, it is easy for any human being to identify what kind of activity is in progress if they hear a short stretch of live conversation.

To illustrate this point, one kind of speech-exchange system is the interview, by which is meant any situation where one person is seeking information from another. In one sense the aims of all interviews are similar, yet their structure is very different. No-one would expect to seek therapy and be treated as though they were in a law court, or a police station. What makes the difference? Clients seek help voluntarily. They talk because they know they need help. Therapists' main consideration is, or ought to be, the welfare of their clients. In a law-court or police station the main consideration is not the well-being of the client although that could be part of a humane procedure. The aim is to get information that the interviewee may not wish to disclose. Here the welfare of the individual is secondary to the need to solve a crime against society. Hence the whole procedure will be different.

Sacks initiated a radically new methodology whose aim was to reveal the unrecognised and unwritten laws that make possible the production of intelligible conversation. We make use of universal unwritten rules that we do not know we know. They have come into being through the need of the human race to develop a more efficient way of communicating. Sacks' interest in how talk worked in the calls received in the suicide centre led him to extend his reading to the study of psychological texts. His enquiring mind and open-minded approach encouraged him to read critically and to ask questions.

This new model for therapy talk that emerged in my findings provides an opportunity for lay people to make sense of psychotherapy for themselves, and for professionals to learn to improve their relationships with clients by eschewing any inappropriate use of power through understanding the process of talk-in-interaction. A new form of collaborative cooperation emerged as I continued to analyse the dialogue: one that recognises the importance of mutual respect between the participants and avoids the unfair use of power. This model can be transposed to all situations where people are trying to solve problems in an attempt to understand each other through acknowledging individual differences through looking at what they have in common rather than what splits them apart.[3]

The most likely motivation for the development of writing may well have been the desire to anchor the oral tradition in a more permanent form. Trying to break down the sounds of speech into recognisable units such as words and sentences must have been a formidable task. Similarly, the abstraction of the form of language, the study of grammar, must have been extremely difficult. It could not have happened until our ancestors had developed both speech and writing and all the skills that derived therefrom to enable them to make their lives easier and to give them the leisure to explore the world of ideas in greater depth.

The language revolution

Although we do not know how people learned to talk we can gain some clues by observing how babies learn. They start with nouns, naming the objects around them. Then they turn to actions, so that they can connect verbs, doing words, with objects, e.g. "drink milk" and "doggie bark". Later they need to be more precise through the use of describing words, like adjectives and adverbs, e.g., "black cat" and "barking loudly". They do not have to know about grammar to do this. Grammatical structure arose, as does all structure, from the need to make something work.

Until the late nineteenth century the study of language was limited to the analysis of its sentence structure, the categorisation of different types of words by labels that defined their functions, primarily nouns, verbs, adverbs and adjectives, and their placement in individual sentences. This is one kind of grammar. Grammarians believed that if they could analyse the structure of sentences, then they could apply the same principles to the analysis of whole conversations. They failed to take into account two factors, the social purpose of language and the psychological differences between the participants. Therefore it was not enough to know about the organisation of the words. Harvey Sacks finally opened up the beginnings of a revolutionary methodology by formulating the following questions. How do we know how to talk with each other? What are the mechanisms by which we understand each other's **utterances** and work together to make mutual sense of them in such a way that we are able to cooperate successfully in a common task? This new insight opened the way to a new approach to the understanding of the structure of therapy talk that eases the task of the diagnosis and treatment of clients' problems.

How do interlocutors manage to collaborate in the undertaking of any social task through the medium of language? The effect of the activity in which they are involved actually governs the style of the talk-in-interaction. Words do not constitute a tool in themselves. We need to understand what people do with them to get what they want. This was Harvey Sacks' unique discovery. Just as Chomsky discovered that children possess an innate ability to work out grammatical structure for themselves, so **members** of society use a set of social rules that they have developed for themselves, largely unconsciously, absorbing them from their talking environment.

The ambivalence of words

The grammarians assumed that words themselves had definable meanings. It was this assumption that made possible the construction of dictionaries. Even so, it was recognised that words could have more than one meaning.[4] The word 'mean' can not only signify 'to make sense of' but can also be used in the sense of 'average' or 'miserly'. Because of the work of Wittgenstein (1953) and Harvey Sacks (1992) we now know that the meaning of words is contingent upon their **context**. Moreover, new meanings for existing words are continuously coming into existence as new technologies develop. In everyday conversation, speech-users love to play about with words and allocate different meanings to them; for example, teenagers, ever on the lookout for ways of rebelling against received opinion, have taken such a word as 'wicked' and transformed it to describe something exciting and desirable. Language is constantly changing because the world is in a continuous state of change and language is the currency of understanding. By the same token, we are all in a constant state of physical and mental change because of the effect of experiences and time on our bodies and our minds. In addition the result of individual, internal adaptations to physiological and emotional changes affect how we respond to external influences.

The concept that words have meaning in themselves fell into disrepute first of all through the work of Ferdinand de Saussure.[5] He recognised that words were arbitrary signs. He demonstrated the difference between the word itself, the sign, and the object it represented, the 'referent'. His work led to the development of semiology, a new body of knowledge concerned with the study of signs.

The importance of dialogue

Meanwhile, in Russia, working under difficulties because of the rigidity of the Stalinist regime, Mikhail Mikhailovich Bakhtin (1981) in the first half of the twentieth century produced a seminal body of work that did not see the light of day in the West until the 1980s. He looked at language as a whole by recognising the connection between speech in talk-in-interaction, and the written word as manifested in literary genres. He defined speech as the primary form of language, and writing as the secondary. Bakhtin developed the idea of speech genres, or styles of speaking that varied according to the speaker.

Bakhtin and Sacks, working in different countries and at different times with no possibility of knowing anything about each other were the first two researchers to recognise the overwhelming importance of dialogue and its particular contribution to the creation of meaning. The main difference between them was that Sacks studied live conversation, the primary use of language, and Bakhtin's interest lay in the secondary use of dialogue in literature. During periods of great change, it often happens that minds working in isolation come up with the same new ideas. There are many similarities between Sacks' and Bakhtin's discoveries.

Dialogue was recognised as a joint activity constructed by two people working together to understand each other. We all have our own view of the world, gathered as a result of the interaction of our innate genetic character and the social environment in which we mature from helpless babies to potentially responsible adults. These differences between individuals lead to difficulties in communication. Every statement made by one person has an effect on the recipient. In ongoing dialogue where both parties are paying attention to each other, which is far from always the case, we learn something new about ourselves and each other all the time.[6]

Dialogue is a continuous search for meaning. Everyday dialogue is disjunctive, full of hesitations, self and other corrections, and delaying tactics that give us time to think and take things in. That is why such particles as 'er', 'um', 'you see', 'well', crop up so frequently. One of the reasons we fail to be conscious of this process is because of the influence of plays where dialogue is constructed, worked and reworked to produce the right dramatic effect. They are far more fluent and understandable than everyday talk, which is an ongoing activity that involves spontaneous, on-the-spot, immediate, creative activity.[7]

The overlapping of boundaries

Aristotle laid the foundations for the academic study of separate sciences in an abstract form as distinct from folklore knowledge based on observation and experience. The mystery of the mind was solved by giving it a new label, soul, and regarding it as a disembodied entity that survived after death. Because we are capable of logical thought, it was assumed that emotions and sensory perceptions played no part in thinking. It took 2000 years for psychologists like Freud, and philosophers like Korzybski (1933), Bertrand Russell (1990), Wittgenstein (1953) and social-linguists like Lakoff (1987) to recognise that we cannot separate thinking from our bodily and emotional experiences.

Korzybski (1933) working in America, was creating a new paradigm to show the connections between different kinds of studies that were formerly seen as separated from each other. This coming together was based on the realisation that it was impossible to treat mind and body as unrelated entities. Whilst this seems blindingly obvious, we need to remember that it is the things that are right under our noses that we fail to see, as both Sacks and Wittgenstein were aware. Thinking is dependent on how we perceive the world around us from our own unique viewpoint. There is no such thing as objectivity. Every researcher influences and is part of their own research.

This realisation led to a major shift of approach in research methods. The value of traditional quantitative research methods, which were concerned with counting, measuring and using questionnaires, was beginning to be questioned. Qualitative methodology is based on a different approach. The researcher affects the research and vice-versa. The old assumption that researchers have inside knowledge and the subjects they were studying played no active part in the outcome is rejected.

Underpinning this change is the recognition of an unacceptable imbalance of power between researcher and subject. The qualitative approach is particularly well-suited to my own research because it recognises that unless clients play an active part in the resolution of a problem, by talking frankly about their particular difficulties, therapists cannot make use of their own acquired professional skills. Clients find their own answers when they make their own use of therapists' guidance.

It seems that it is only when bodies of knowledge have reached a certain level of sophistication that we can begin to think about how they connect with each other. We can understand the meaning of the whole picture only when we understand the meaning of the parts. Analysis precedes synthesis. In the western world the early twentieth century was the right time. The domain of social science had come into being as a result of the growing sense of outrage felt by a few responsible people about the miserable living conditions of the majority of the population. The hold of religious beliefs, especially those that promised people the prospect of a reward for their sufferings after death, were beginning to lose their grip. There was a growing feeling that we could improve the human condition in this life through our own efforts without having to wait for divine intervention.

A powerful catalyst for this change was the new ideas that were being minted by the developments in psychology initiated by people like William James and Sigmund Freud. Freud's formulation of psychoanalysis was the first system developed for the exploration of the psychological causes of human suffering.

Korzybski (1933) proposed that there is a connection between how we use language and sanity. This comes about because we confuse the sign (the word) with what it stands for. We think of the word as an object in itself. This gives us the impression that we understand its meaning. This is only partly true. If we hear the word 'dog' it is true we will summon up an image of a dog in our minds, but everyone's image will be different, according to what they know about dogs.

Bateson (1972) was a polymath whose wide background enabled him to make connections within different disciplines. Like Korzybski, he opined that the inappropriate use of language could be a factor in the development of some kinds of mental illness. In psychotherapy, clients frequently present their problems in phrases such as low self-esteem, lack of confidence, or depression that they have gleaned from the media and self-help books. These lexical phrases and items do not define a factual state. They are all summaries of a cluster of symptoms that are different for each individual. They mean nothing on their own, because clients use these labels as an approximate description of inner states of mind. When a client tells me "I've got depression" unless they tell me how they have come to that decision, I have no information at all. Therefore in psychotherapy one of the main tasks is to encourage clients to describe the symptoms that they are experiencing in their own language.

Sacks notes that one of Freud's difficulties was that "everybody considered themselves to be an authority in psychology" (Sacks, 1992, p. 202). This is because in common parlance people use the word 'depression' to describe many different states of feeling temporarily miserable. In medical language depression is used as a term for a 'mental illness'. Hence there is confusion about the meaning of the term, and by labelling themselves as 'depressed' clients can come to believe that they are suffering an illness and are no more responsible for their state of mind than they are for catching 'flu'. Once a label is accepted as a state of illness, there is no incentive for the patient to take responsibility for trying to put matters right for themselves (Simeons, 1960, Szaz, 1972). This is not to say that there is no such thing as mental illness. Of course there is. But because of the nebulous nature of emotions, it is extremely difficult for both psychiatrists and psychotherapists to distinguish between neurosis from which we all suffer to a greater or lesser degree, and psychosis. Psychosis is the new word for what we used to call 'madness'. From my own experience I believe that psychotic people are so far removed from reality that psychotherapy does not work for them.

Korzybski (1933) argues that the long period of two thousand years since the times of Aristotle during which mind and body were seen as separate entities is now at an end. The mind is dependent on the body, and the body on the mind. Health depends on how realistically we manage our lives. We can talk ourselves into a state of ill-health through the way we organise our inner and spoken dialogue and beliefs. Despite the fact that hypochondriac behaviour and its causes are common knowledge and have long been understood by everybody (there are many examples in the literature of all countries) we still use words in a way that undermines our powers to take control of our own lives.

*The effect of the silent revolution on the practice
of psychotherapy*

The silent revolution has moved from a position where the structure of language, both spoken and written, and the meaning of words were fixed entities to a new view that recognises the importance of what we do with language when we are speaking with each other and what that tells us about the structure of the mind itself and of the structure of our social behaviour.

A further important change is the recognition that syntax and semantics in language, which means structure and form in a general sense, cannot be separated because they have an ongoing interactive effect on each other. For example, the structure of a tree is determined by its need for nourishment through air, water and sun and the particular place where it grows. If the nourishment is insufficient, and/or the tree is growing too close to others, its final fully developed form will be recognisable as a tree, but it will be distorted. It is the same with people. We need the best possible environment in order to make the optimum use of our potential.

By the same token whatever particular social activity in which we are engaged produces a particular style of structure; and that structure itself reveals the nature of the activity. If we were given a transcript taken from a certain context, such as a court of law for instance, it would not take us long to recognise the nature of the context, without prior knowledge. The style of the verbal interchange would make it clear.

Sacks' approach to conversation as a social activity required a new vocabulary. Grammatical terms are not of much use to us when we aim to understand what people are doing when they talk together. The application of CA methodology made the invention of new technical terms a necessity. This terminology helps us to think differently about what we do when we are talking together.

From now on, instead of using the terms 'word' or 'phrase' I shall refer to **lexical items**. I shall replace 'sentence', defined in grammar as a group of different types of words such as verbs, nouns and adjectives arranged in a certain order that produces a comprehensible whole, with the term **utterance**. An utterance in CA is a conversational **turn**. When one person speaks, whether they say one word or several sentences, that is an utterance. It is a useful way of helping us to think of an utterance as an individual contribution to joint talk, however short or long it may be. It might be a single word reply 'Oh', or it might be several sentences long. Meaning is transmitted not through individual sentences, but through the sense of a complete utterance, which can vary from a group of several sentences to a single word. Bakhtin posited that an utterance could constitute a complete novel.

Conclusion

This chapter is a very brief account of the changes in thinking that underpin the CA approach to conversation. I have called this a silent revolution because most people are unaware of these changes and continue to use long-established and ineffective ways of communicating. I believe that much useful research sits in university libraries and does not percolate down to everyday life. Throughout this book I am continuously aware of my aim to write as simply as possible and yet not to over-simplify. Sacks' ideas are particularly valuable because he saw the connections between language and psychotherapy.

I believe, along with many others, that much human misery is caused because we have over-idealistic expectations of how life should be. These expectations are reflected in how we speak to each other. In order to know what we need to change in our way of conducting conversation, we need first to understand what is going on. This book aims to clarify for readers some of the ways we use language to help us to get what we need to make the most of our lives. We can then examine which of these strategies work and which ones do not. Proposals for what does work are illustrated from my audio recordings of therapy sessions.

We begin in the second chapter with the reasons why we bother to talk to each other at all; and how even the simplest verbal exchange can cause trouble.

NOTES

1. Chomsky's seminal work demolished the notion, beloved of the behaviourists, that environment is all and inborn characteristics count for little. He argued that language was not just picked up from hearing the spoken language around us by means of a

stimulus-response system. This would lead only to "a system of habits, a network of associations. And such a system will not account for the sound-meaning relation that all of us know intuitively when we have mastered a language." (Cogswell & Gordon, 1996, p. 60). The work done in the late twentieth century on evolutionary psychology, cognitive processes, and the knowledge of genes and how they function brought together the related sciences of biology, psychology, sociology and neurology, in the recognition that the old nature/nurture argument was demolished once and for all and due importance was give to our genetic inheritance. It is not a case of either/or. There is an ongoing recursive learning process through the continuous interaction between our inborn characteristics and the ever-changing environment.

2. The link between structure, content and function is very important not only for CA but for many other domains. An important and beautifully written book on this subject is Christopher Alexander's book *"Notes on the Synthesis of Form"*.

3. Edward de Bono (1985) wrote a book on conflicts and how to resolve them, based on his theory of lateral thinking. He proposed that we need to move beyond conflict to a higher level of creative thinking, which would work out to the satisfaction of all parties involved.

4. One of the ways that the outdated grammarian approach still manifests itself is in the general assumption that words have an exact meaning. This can be particularly harmful in the case of certain kinds of diagnosis. Diagnoses are not facts but opinions based on professional knowledge. If they were facts there would be no such thing as misdiagnoses. Since medical knowledge of how the body works is immeasurably more advanced that psychological knowledge, it is not wise to accept unconditionally a diagnosis of 'depression' for example. It is a term used in psychiatry for a collection of symptoms that are revised every now and then as new knowledge comes to light. Many of these symptoms are normal for everyone when life gets particularly difficult for us. In many cases the answer is not to treat it as an illness but to understand the underlying causes. Psychotherapy is particularly useful for treating such cases, provided always those clients are willing to recognise the importance of their response to difficult situations and work towards changing them.

5. Ferdinand de Saussure was born in Switzerland in 1857 and died in 1913. He was a specialist in the ancient Sanskrit language. When he was appointed to a chair at the University of Geneva in 1891 he was asked to teach a course on general linguistics. Although he was reluctant to do so, because of the difficulty of

the subject, he embarked on a new approach and taught it to his students as he redeveloped his ideas, instead of relying on old lecture notes. He established a new method, semiology, which took as its basic premise that words should be seen as signs representing objects. His findings were acclaimed by his students and influenced other European linguists which led to his becoming known in America.

6. One of the ways in which we get to know ourselves is in our dialogues with others, provided that we are willing to make sense of our own reactions, both cognitive and emotional. For example, if we find that we are easily irritated, it may be because we are impatient or closed-minded. We cannot know about our own inherited nature unless we interact with others. We cannot be kind or cruel, loving or unfeeling, generous or mean in a vacuum. Thus in every interaction with other people we learn to understand ourselves better, and this is the first requirement for beginning to understand other people and the ways in which they are different from ourselves.

7. Every dialogue with another person is fresh and unrehearsed. It becomes less so when we know that other person well and have established patterns of talking with them. However, having established patterns does not mean that we are talking in the most mutually cooperative way. Psychotherapy identifies the patterns and helps clients to see what are useful and which need to be changed to improve their quality of life.

CHAPTER TWO

The purpose of conversation and its link with psychotherapy

In this chapter I shall discuss two themes: the purpose of conversation as social action, and the state of psychotherapy today as a start to making the connections between Sacks' views of conversation and the changes that have taken place in the way psychotherapy is understood today.

The purpose of conversation

Why do we talk to each other? Why do many of us have difficulty talking to strangers? Why do so many conversations end up in fruitless arguments? Why is it we often feel thrown off balance by what another person says to us? Why is it easier to talk with people when there is some distance between us, and much more difficult when we live in close proximity? As a practising psychotherapist I have ample evidence that many people would like to know the answers to these questions. This book is intended to provide the foundation of more research into the subtleness of conversation.

There are good reasons for people to be nervous about talking to others. All conversations are fraught with difficulties because of the particular way we make sense of the world. Each one of us has our own unique genetic inheritance. Each of us reacts differently to the environment. We all know that children brought up in a similar way by the same parents can grow up to be very different people. Stephen Pinker (2002) makes an excellent case for the supremacy of nature over nurture, and, at the same time, he does not underestimate the important part played by the environment.

We all need to be exposed to a community in order for our inherent characteristics to develop, yet we all have different needs. Hence no upbringing is perfect. Whatever its faults, any kind of human influence, especially during the early years, is better than none. For instance the brain can learn languages easily only up to a certain age. If we do not hear people talking around us and to us before that age, whatever kind of talk it is, we shall never acquire a natural fluency and understanding of our native tongue.

There are two kinds of dialogue, those where two can play and those we conduct with ourselves. For the moment we are concerned with the first. When we open up an everyday conversation we want something from another person. There can be many reasons. The main categories are:

a) Talking to show others we are friendly
b) Talking to show others we are unfriendly
c) Talking to be reminded
d) Talking to get information
e) Talking to get cooperation
f) The inner dialogue

(a & b) Phatic talk

When I was young I used to despise small-talk. For a long time I failed to recognise what it was for. Sacks shows us that **phatic talk**, although it has little or no content, *does* have a social purpose. Categories (a) and (b) in particular can be vehicles for phatic talk. Just as dogs make friendly and unfriendly approaches to each other through body posturing, human beings do the equivalent with speech and body language:

(1)
```
A Nice day isn't it?
B Lovely! Good to see the sun.
```

(2)
```
A Hello
B Hello
```

This type of interchange is called a greeting. That is its social pur-pose. It is an example of the type of two-**turn** verbal exchanges that Sacks calls **adjacency pairs**: the basic unit for conversation. They comprise two conversational **turns**. It takes two to tango. An **adja-cency pair** is complete in itself, as in the two examples above.

The first turn in adjacency pairs constrains another person to reply. A lack of response can be disconcerting for the first speaker. There may be a perfectly good reason why the respondent does not answer. That person may not have heard, or may be lost in a rev-erie. However, such is the powerful expectation created by the first turn of the adjacency pair, most of the time, the speaker assumes that a lack of response implies that something is wrong. Next time the speaker may hold back from initiating the greeting because of a fear of rejection leading to injured pride. It is not a comfortable matter to believe your friendly approach has been thrown back in your face.

The expected response to a greeting like 'hello' is 'hello'. However, occasionally it happens that the response is indubitably unfriendly:

(3)
```
A Hello
B Get lost
```

No assumptions are needed here. If the first speaker is an unusually direct sort of person he may pursue the matter further in an effort to clear up a difficult situation. If he easily feels slighted he may come back with a belligerent third turn, or he may keep silent and harbour a smouldering resentment.

Such is the fear of upsetting another person by confronting a situ-ation and resolving it, that many people build up a bank account of small resentments that can result in a chronically disgruntled attitude to the world. When this resentment is unconscious, i.e., not recognised by the conscious mind, it can result in psychosomatic symptoms, such as phobias of many kinds, compulsive behaviours, and lapses of memory. It is common in psychotherapy to hear accounts of such events, which are usually described by clients as 'silly'. Nothing is silly if it is causing serious distress.

All behaviour has its underlying cause, and the kind of behaviour that results in causing another person to experience malevolent anguish usually has perfectly understandable roots. Psychotherapy can help us to uncover the roots of these feelings, providing we are willing to look inside ourselves for the answers. Once we know why we respond in a certain way we have the tools to help us to change our own behaviour.

Phatic talk reflects our need to belong: to be recognised either as an individual in our own right or to feel part and parcel of a group. People who want to be seen as unfriendly have their reasons. Phatic talk may be initiated in order to show that we are friendly towards another or because we want to initiate a conversation. It is a useful way of maintaining good relationships with friends and acquaintances that involves little effort. The exchange is complete in itself, as all adjacency pairs are. The first speaker then has the option of saying no more or of starting up a conversation. The second option implies that we have something to say that requires a response. We need someone to listen to us.

(c) Talking to be reminded

The need to be heard is a major factor in the popularity of psychotherapy and counselling. Most of us have not been listened to attentively enough in childhood. Children are continually learning new things about the world and the people in it, and are overwhelmed by the need to seek more information from adults. When small children want something they want it now, whether it is a desirable object, or new knowledge. Learning to wait for anything, including their turn to speak, is not something children do naturally.

Children have not yet learned the rules of etiquette in conversation. Like all of us, they only learn through the gradual recognition that if they do not listen to other people then they will themselves not be listened to. They have yet to master the art of timing, which is itself the result of paying attention to the responses of others.

For instance, no-one wants to be interrupted whilst cooking by an insistent voice three feet above the ground demanding an immediate answer to "If God is everywhere why don't we bump into him?".[1] Deferred gratification, the ability to wait, is something that we learn gradually (hopefully) as we mature. Parents do not have to be perfect, which is just as well since none of us are, but if we listen enough, our children may be less likely to grow up into over-demanding adults.

In psychotherapy training much lip-service is paid to the value of listening to clients. However, we are not taught how to listen. Harvey Sacks' experience in researching audio recordings at the Center for the Scientific Study of Suicide in Los Angeles aroused his interest in what callers wanted from counsellors. He cited Fromm-Reichmann's (1960) advice to trainee psychoanalysts not to talk about their own experiences to clients. She advocated that they should learn 'how not to be reminded' of their own experiences. Sacks concluded that to ask therapists to try not to be reminded is to ask them to behave unnaturally.

Sacks' experience at the Centre revealed that a routine complaint of patients was that their psychiatrists didn't understand them; that they "didn't want psychiatrists but people who have had similar experience" (Sacks, 1992, p. 771). Sacks opined that people listen to be reminded of their own experiences, and that this is a powerful incentive to listening. He did not see how people could learn not to be reminded. He proposed that if therapists were making a conscious effort to suppress the surfacing of their own past experiences, then perhaps that was a good enough reason for the common complaint of clients that psychiatrists sometimes fall asleep during consultations.

Sacks realised that what we hear can only be understood in the light of our own view of the world. Whatever is said to us triggers off a train of our personal memories, whether we like it or not. There are at least two ways of responding. We can seize the opportunity to launch into a self-centred monologue (and we all know how boring that can be for the recipient) or we can offer our own experience as a possibly helpful model for the person we are talking with.

This is an example of how Sacks challenged some of the assumptions about psychotherapy in the 1960s. Yet the myth that therapists should not listen to be reminded lingers on in the profession.

Whenever anyone is telling a story, the nature of the listener's responses encourages the story-teller by demonstrating that they are heard with effortfulness. Thus even a story-telling which involves one person doing most of the talking is jointly produced. The aptness or inaptness of the responses demonstrates to the story-teller whether or not the listener is paying attention to what is being said.

We do not have to have any knowledge of psychological theory to know when we are not being listened to. Clients soon notice if we fail to remember something they told us before. One of the difficulties for therapists is that when they have, perhaps, thirty cases on their books, it requires a considerable effort on their part to remember everyone's details. Fortunately, as long as we have established a good rapport with them, they will forgive us if we make the odd mistake. The secret of listening to another in order to encourage that other to feel heard and understood is to focus all one's attention on that person. I propose that in everyday life this is a rare occurrence, and therefore something that we all crave. Research has shown that the amount of empathy felt by the mother to the baby is a sure guide to the degree of the management of satisfying relationships in adult life.

(d) Talking to get information

This category can be, like greetings, the simplest kind of speech-exchange, an adjacency pair. One person asks for something, e.g., directions in a strange place, and the other person responds. There is no need for the conversation to go further. A request for information may have hidden implications that confuse the issue of knowing how to respond. It may be an oblique way of getting to know someone.

In the early stages of psychotherapy, information gathering plays an important part. Clients expect to tell stories about their difficulties and the first task of therapists is to encourage them to talk. This kind of story-telling is called troubles-telling. There is a dichotomy here since although clients are paying for a service to help them to identify and solve a problem, they are naturally nervous of giving away too much about themselves too early. They need to reach a point when they can feel they trust the therapist.

Clients tell their stories from their own point of view, which means they tell them in such a way that conveys the impression they want to give to the therapist. This process is called **gloss** in CA terminology. What we call it has been labelled **spin** in other domains, especially in politics. When we are talking to one person or to an audience we always have in mind the purpose of that talk. Therefore therapists need to be acutely aware at all times of the clues clients give whilst troubles-telling. Such clues are important for the identification of the problem the client may either be unaware of or may be reluctant to reveal. The chapter on **troubles-telling** will reveal the difference between story-telling in ordinary conversation and troubles-telling in therapy.

(e) Talking to get cooperation

Most talk that is not phatic comes into this category: asking for help, opening up a discussion, trying to persuade another, managing a small child, negotiating a business deal, teaching, psychotherapy. All are different forms of social action involving at least two people. The word cooperation is a generalisation that can have many different meanings. We ask for cooperation when we want something for ourselves, e.g., when we want someone to do us a favour; when we want to carry out some social activity that will benefit a group and need to find people who want to be in such a group, e.g., setting up a committee; when we have a job to do, such as teaching, where we need the cooperation of our students; and of course psychotherapy, where no work can be done without clients' committed involvement.

All these activities involve the exercise of our own powers to persuade other/s. Whenever the subject of power arises ethical considerations have to be taken into account. Power is all too often thought of as a tyrannical tool to coerce others into doing what they do not want to do; and indeed it is often used in this way. Yet without the judicious use of our personal powers to influence, we cannot carry out the tasks we set ourselves. Power is neutral, in the same sense that money is neutral. It is the motivation behind the use of power that determines whether it is beneficial or destructive. In simple terms when we influence others by what we say, and we cannot avoid doing so, that influence is most beneficial when it helps others to think things out for themselves, rather than attempting to convert them to our own point of view.

When psychotherapy works, therapists use their powers for several different purposes: to encourage clients to feel at ease in their company; to make it easy for clients to talk freely, without restraint; to use all **interventions**, whether they be interpretations, suggestions, information and elements from their own professional and personal experience, as tools to help clients to make use of their own resources and come to their own conclusions about what is best for them. This goal is not easily achieved. Therapists are not saintly beings who find it easy to be non-judgemental and full of unconditional regard for their clients: one of the requirements laid down by Carl Rogers (1957) and a fundamental tenet of counselling. No human beings could fulfil such an ideal, nor is it desirable that they should.

Holstein & Gubrium (1997, p. 120) stress the importance of creative interviewing. Whatever the task of the interviewer, be it psychotherapy or research, the interviewers should be aware of their own reactions:

> "Continual self-analysis on the part of the interviewer, who usually is also the researcher, is necessary, lest the creative interviewer's own defence mechanisms work against mutual disclosure and understanding."

In all relationships there are misunderstandings and feelings of irritation. The secret is not to pretend they do not exist but to acknowledge them to oneself without self-judgement and without venting one's annoyance openly in an aggressive way. This is a vital element in the achievement of cooperation.

(f) The inner dialogue

Whatever we are doing, whenever we are engaged in conversation, there is an ongoing dialogue taking place within us. We may not be consciously aware of it, but it manifests itself in a benevolent form when it enables us to talk to others in a way that shows we respect and like them and in a negative form when it is displayed through speech and body language as irritability, inappropriate annoyance with others, indecision and its close relation procrastination. A good example of procrastination in Shakespeare is Hamlet's soliloquy, "To be or not to be, that is the question". To make a decision whether to live or die causes problems when it is based on a choice between two powerfully negative feelings: not being able to come to terms with everyday living and being afraid of what will happen after death.

Nothing is written in stone. Nothing is black or white. Our sense of identity and the way we think is the result of the continuous inter-action between our genetic inheritance and our life experiences (see Chapter Four). We are often confused when making decisions because we are able to see more than one point of view. There is nothing wrong with confusion—it shows that we are able to remain open-minded. We can console ourselves that much harm in the world is done by people who believe they are right.

Constant self-analysis may or may not be useful. Wittgenstein showed us that 'thinking' is extraordinarily difficult to define. No-one knows how we manage to do it. Many confuse it with what Yapko (1989) calls 'rumination', an unhelpful device that involves going over the same material again and again, yet failing to get any results because some of the key elements that would help us to come to a realistic conclusion are missing. We are constantly growing and developing and when we make changes we cannot know before-hand what the results will be. We can make imaginary scenarios about the future, but until we are involved in a new situation we cannot be certain about how we will react to it.

One of the purposes of psychotherapy is to help us to find these missing elements. We are all blind to certain aspects of ourselves, for understandable reasons, mainly because of our wish to be seen in a certain way by others. If there are any facets of ourselves that we dis-like we tend to repress them to the point that we are not consciously aware of them. One of Freud's many discoveries is that although this may be the case, it is impossible for us to prevent evidence of our repressions from breaking through into our talk with others. An important aspect of common knowledge is that most of us under-stand what is meant by the phrase 'Freudian slip'.

The present state of psychotherapy

Freud's (1915e, 1923) work was seminal inasmuch as it constituted the construction of the first complete system of psychotherapy. This is psychoanalysis which still flourishes today although changes have occurred, as is to be expected, since its inception. Whilst certain aspects of his work have been justly criticised, his findings about the dynamics of human nature, especially the related hypotheses of the unconscious mind and the personality structure of the id, ego and superego created a framework that proved to be very helpful for the understanding of human behaviour. The speed at which his method flourished could be seen as an overwhelming sign of the need for such a discipline.

He was the first to create a practical system for helping people to find the source of their dissatisfactions with life and open up for them the possibility of personal change. Freud's method was authoritarian and therapist led. The patient talked at length and the doctor said little, except for interventions and information-giving. This was based on the belief that the therapist should be a blank screen on which the patients' problems could be projected.

Freud dealt with the individual and the effects of the childhood environment on present behaviour. However, he left out the effects of the patients' social environment and of people's need to find some meaning in their lives that transcended their day-to-day existence. Adler (Lundin, 1989) supplied the former and Jung (1959) the latter. The picture was then complete and provided a sound basis for all those who followed after.

For a long period of the 20th century, behaviourism, the approach that believed we could change people by social engineering, based on the premise that environment is more important than inherited characteristics, was very popular. However, with the advent of the revolutionary changes in thinking that I have briefly discussed in the last chapter, all this changed as a result of the studies on artificial intelligence and especially the new domains of cognitive science, evolutionary psychology and genetics. It is now generally recognised that how individuals develop depends on the particular interaction of each individual's genetic inheritance with their environment (see Chapter Four).

In the last century psychotherapy has proliferated and many new approaches have been devised resulting in the existence of some 400 different systems (Feltham, 2000). This has presented great difficulties for the understanding of how psychotherapy works.

The development of the humanistic approach

Rogers (1957, 1990), the originator of counselling, produced a model he called client-centred therapy. He believed that therapists' self-understanding and openness could set an example. Clients could begin to expand those qualities in themselves and face the sometimes perilous exploration of their inner world with less fear. Rogers' method is based on a non-judgemental, respectful attitude towards clients. McGuiness (2000, p. 94) states that there is overwhelming agreement in the profession that:

> "the key factor in client change resides in the relationship between client and therapist, and in the 'self' that the therapist is able to put into a relationship with the client."

This agreement was initially recognised by Jung, who believed that each patient should be treated as an individual. He avoided routine approaches: "The crucial point is that I confront the patient as one human being to another." (Jung 1961, p. 130–131) He recognised that both patient and doctor underwent personal change in the process of therapy.

This movement away from the authoritarianism of Freud, where the process of therapy is managed in a therapist-directed way in which the therapist takes pains not to reveal information about his own life, culminated into what has been called the existential humanistic model. This model is consonant with the idea of the therapeutic alliance, a form of cooperative interaction, which results in both participants playing an active part in the therapeutic work.

This major trend in psychotherapy is pervasive over a wide range of therapeutic models. Bohart and Tallman emphasise that looking at "the whole person's struggle to make his or her life work" is basically different from what the authors call "part-person models" such as cognitive therapy that "sees dysfunctional schemas as the cause of problems" and behaviour therapy that "views problems as dysfunctional habits". (Bohart and Tallman, 1996, p. 10)

However I would argue that this is not a case of either/or. All models could be useful for particular purposes. Each person's struggle to overcome difficulties presents different problems requiring different solutions. An essential skill needed for successful therapy is therapists' ability to make the best choices from their store of knowledge and experience to suit individual needs. Some therapists, myself included, take an eclectic approach and continue to add to their toolboxes by exploring different models.

Harvey Sacks, throughout his lecture notes displays his thirst for knowledge and his open-mindedness, coming up with his own conclusions, based on acute observations of the process of therapy: about people's real needs, rather than their unrealistic wants. In this book I aim to make the fullest use of these deductions, since they were often the catalysts that led me to understand some aspect of working with clients that I had not fully grasped.

Conclusion

In this chapter I have examined the different reasons why we talk to each other and the relation of talk to the way psychotherapy is practised today. The next chapter will focus on how we make sense of ourselves, other people and objects in the external world: the foundation on which we build the structure of conversation.

The following schema is a summary of the basic changes in the practice of psychotherapy that we have discussed in the last two chapters:

From	→ Towards
Therapist-directed	→ Cooperation between therapist and client
Esoteric	→ Exoteric
(available to a selected few)	(available to many)
Deductive	→ Inductive
(top-down, theory-based)	(bottom-up)

The next chapter explores how we make sense of the world we live in and form some common conclusion about the way things are. Without such guide-lines it would be very difficult to conduct a conversation at all.

NOTE

1. This question was asked by a five-year-old in a class taught by my sister when she was a young teacher just out of college. Mary had the foresight to write down some of the children's questions, when the freshness and originality of perception and thought of small children made a great impact on her.

CHAPTER THREE

Economy—The key to the practice of conversation

There are two fundamental characteristics that, to a greater or lesser degree, underpin all human behaviour. One is to prefer the status quo, and the other to restrict action to those things we want and need to do. The paradox of managing our lives can only be resolved by finding a balance between holding on to the creative strategies we have learned from the past, and playing an active part in making use of inevitable changes to enhance our lives, rather than seeing ourselves as the passive victims of change. The adage "better the devil you know than the devil you don't know" epitomises this problem. It has always taken courage to face the unknown, whether it is uncharted external territories, or the depths of our unique selves. How often do we look back on past actions and find it almost impossible to remember why they seemed so important to us at the time? Freud's profound statement that we are under the influence of inner forces of which we are largely unaware is all too true.

How we do the best for ourselves in the 'here and now', depends on two factors, first, our genetic inheritance, and second, the way we develop our potential to be able to learn from our experiences what we need to know to make the best use of our lives. This is very difficult to do alone, although some brave souls manage it, because we all have blind spots about certain aspects of ourselves that we shy away from examining. It takes specialists in psychological theory and experience who have themselves undergone the examination of their own lives with another professional, to be able to carry out the same process with other people.

The more we know about ourselves, the more we develop the ability to accept all aspects of our beings which leads to an increasing capacity to take responsibility for our lives and let other people get on with their own. It is only when we have undergone this process that are we fit to give other people the support and help they need in a non-blaming way. The influence we have as psychotherapists is of the kind that helps others to find their own powers and use them wisely. If we use it to force others to agree with us, whether they want to or not, then that power is used to oppress and will have the effect of weakening their already precarious sense of themselves. On the other hand, to collude, to agree with clients' distorted view of themselves or others, is dishonest and counter-productive. How we manage to avoid arguments and yet use our powers to help people to understand their own actions are a mark of the therapist's natural and learned skills. This is why I see psychotherapy as an art rather than a science.

I start with the assumption that we have learned to conduct conversations with each other, as we learn to do everything when we first attempt it, in the easiest and quickest way to get results. This is essential. It enables us to actually get started and have a go. However, when we stay with the stereotypical idea that this is how conversation is, we find that as we get deeper into a relationship with another person, difficulties arise precisely because of the short cuts that enable us to talk with ease. It is these very short cuts that get in the way when we are doing a different kind of conversation, the therapeutic dialogue. In order to clarify these points I shall explore the following topics:

* How we make sense of the world through **categorisation**.
* Economy in conversation.
* The demands of the social task of psychotherapy.

How we make sense of the world through categorisation

(a) How a baby learns to categorise

Categorisation is of primary importance for all human activities. It is the way we learn to understand about similarities and differences. When we are born, we are not aware of our separateness. All the world is one and we are at its centre. As our brains develop one of the first things we notice is that food does not appear magically when we are hungry, someone has to bring it to us. Thus our first categorisation is that we are all part of a group where what we all have in common is separateness. Once that has been established we can then begin to notice what external objects we have in common so that we can make connections between them.

We can imagine some of the difficulties babies encounter when they are learning to speak. They cannot learn to talk unless they are surrounded by live talk. They learn such things as lexical labels for objects by listening and repeating. But as Chomsky (Cook & Newson, 1998) demonstrated, the way they put words in a meaningful order and modify verbs to make past and future tenses, shows that they have an innate language faculty which enables them to work out what makes sense and what does not. It is precisely this capacity that distinguishes human speech from that of talking birds for example.

The failure to get things right at the first attempt is part of the process of learning, and a valuable one. Errors often turn out to be 'intelligent mistakes' that display children's ability to make deductions from what they already know. They soon recognise that they can change the present tense of a regular verb into the past tense by adding the suffix '-ed' to the root. They receive constant feedback from adults when they do not get it right first time. Through taking in talk around them, and learning from feedback, they begin to recognise that some verbs have different suffixes. Stephen Pinker (1995) notes that correction by parents is often ignored by small children. They work out for themselves the peculiarities of irregular verbs, apparently by a process of osmosis through direct experience: a reinforcement of Chomsky's discovery of the universal innate language faculty.

When speech was invented and names given to objects, events, and feelings it became possible to define differences and similarities in a concrete form: the first steps in building categories. When my second son began to make identifiable noises, he used one **lexical item** for several different objects. That word was 'iggle-iggle'. I began to see connections between the objects he identified in this way: plates, cotton reels, the sun and the wheels on his favourite toy cars. At eighteen months he found a short cut of his own by categorising very different things through one element they all shared. The philosopher Wittgenstein (1953) would have understood what my son was doing. He was seeing family resemblances between these different kinds of 'iggle-iggle'. Although these objects had little in common they shared one feature. They were all round in shape.

It is easy to take the act of talking for granted. It must require a lot of practice for babies to adapt the muscles of the mouth to the production of the peculiarities of our native language. The 'wh' phoneme is one that babies learn after they have mastered those that require the use of fewer muscles such as 'm' and 'd'. This is something I learned empirically when attempting to understand what my own babies were trying to say.

My son's sense of priorities in learning language revolved around the production of lexical items to describe his favourite objects. By applying the terminology 'iggle-iggle' to all kinds of things that had nothing to do with machinery, he was developing his own language in a way that reflected his main interest.[1] I realised how difficult it must be for babies to begin to separate one object from another, when they are adjusting to a world where they are constantly seeing things for the first time.

Once speech began to develop as a way for people to communicate with each other the need to be able to differentiate between the objects in the world became pressing. People had to find labels for objects that everyone else in their group could understand. If my son had continued to use the term 'iggle-iggle' for all objects that had an element of circularity he would soon have got into deep trouble when other children and adults failed to see what he meant. The private language he evolved for himself, of which 'iggle-iggle' was one example of a stage in the progress towards a more universal method of categorisation. As we grow older we take for granted both the words we use and the objects they describe. Yet we forget that what we take for granted was at one time unknown and had to be discovered or invented.

The process of categorisation is essential in all language use and is a central theme of this book.

(b) Categorisations of objects

George Lakoff describes what categories reveal about the mind. He works in the field of cognitive science:

> "a new field that brings together what is known about the mind from many academic disciplines: psychology, linguistics, anthropology, philosophy, and computer science. It seeks detailed answers to such questions as: What is reason? How do we make sense of our experience? What is a conceptual system and how is it organised? Do all people use the same conceptual system? If so, what is that system? If not, exactly what is there that is common to the way all human beings think?" (Lakoff, 1987, p. xi)

Lakoff's questions enabled him to come to some important conclusions. He discovered that the mind/body connection was reflected in language through the metaphors we use every day. For example, the kind of descriptions we give to describe anger are closely related to our emotional and physiological reactions when we allow ourselves to get angry.

Agitation is expressed by the following phrases:

- She was shaking with anger
- He's all worked up

Similarly, internal pressure can be described as follows:

- When I found out I almost burst a blood vessel

And interference with accurate perception as follows:

- She was blind with rage
- I was beginning to see red (Lakoff, 1987)

Categorisation depends on two factors. First, who is doing the categorising, as we saw in the example above of my son's 'iggle-iggle', and second, it depends on that person's ability to notice similarities.

At the same university (UCLA), Eleanor Rosch and her colleagues (1976) came up with a theory of prototype categories, i.e. the kind of **generalisations** that enable us to describe a large number of objects that have something in common. Rosch proposes that there are three categories that constitute a hierarchy. Here is one example:

Superordinate:	animal	(biggest group)
Prototype (basic level):	dog	(second biggest group)
Subordinates:	labrador	(smallest group)

Prototypes are 'best examples'. For instance, when children begin to talk they learn the names for groups of similar objects such as 'bird'. This is the basic level category because it is the one we learn first. Since most of the birds babies see, in our particular culture, are garden birds, a robin would be a typical example. When taken to the zoo for the first time, small children might see a penguin, and fail to recognise it as a bird because it is very different in appearance and size from the birds they are accustomed to.[2] It is much easier for small children to have one overall name for something they can recognise easily and quickly. 'Bird' will do very well until their knowledge of the world grows.

Children can then begin to differentiate to a greater degree by naming ostriches, eagles and all other birds that are seen as atypical (subordinate categories). Even later, children begin to realise that birds are part of a much wider category called 'animals', which, according to the stereotypical definition, includes all living creatures other than human beings and plants.[3] It seems that in the initial stages of making sense of the world we need to see more similarities between objects and to look for differences later.

(c) How we categorise ourselves

Just as we categorise objects, so we categorise ourselves and others. How we do this has a powerful and largely unrecognised effect on what happens when we talk together. Our sense of identity is double-faceted. We all have an understanding of ourselves based on the interaction of innate characteristics with aspects of our external environment (other people and the society into which we are born). At the same time most of us construct an idealised image of ourselves that reflects how we want others to see us. Both play a part in our relationships with people. We all find a place for ourselves on the following spectrum:

Realistic self-image —————————— Unrealistic self-image

At one extreme are those who have a high degree of information about both negative and positive aspects of themselves gained from experience that is enhanced by the ability to avoid self-deception. They tend to have the highest degree of confidence, warranted by their ability to make realistic judgements. They have the least need to worry about criticism from others.

At the other extreme are people who have no clear images of themselves and lead their lives carrying out other people's expectations. They are uncertain about what they want, because they have not discovered much about their own potential. They are swayed by the last person they spoke with. They are indecisive, passive, and have not learned that what happens to us is less important than how we deal with it.

Of course there is no-one who exactly fulfils either of these criteria. They are what Lakoff (1987) calls **idealised cognitive models**: **I.C.M.s**. The closer people are to the unrealistic category, the more difficulty they encounter in making satisfactory relationships and decisions about what they want from life. Indecision and procrastination hamper their ability to take action. Most people who seek therapy are closer to the right of the spectrum than to the left. They are not in any way sick, in the medical use of the term, but they are confused.

Without self-understanding we cannot begin to understand others. Trying to give people what we think they want is a good recipe for disaster. No-one will succeed as a therapist without having had the courage to undergo a strict examination of themselves, preferably with another professional person. Talking to friends rarely helps us to understand ourselves better, unless we have exceptionally honest friends who are not afraid to risk the relationship by saying what they really think instead of focusing on keeping us happy. Having a high level of intelligence is not always an advantage. If often means that we have the power to use our minds to construct rationalisations that support the view of ourselves that we wish to retain, sweeping everything else to one side. Freud's work on defence mechanisms shows just how true this is. Their existence is evidence that we all tend to hide from other people, and from ourselves, the very things that we need to understand.

However, because of the constraints of our social environment, we need to be careful not to upset other people (or ourselves) unnecessarily. Erving Goffman (1955) recognises that everyone, to a greater or lesser extent, takes other people's feelings into consideration by doing 'face-saving'; the avoidance of causing unnecessary distress.

Sacks describes another element of communication when he says "Everyone has to lie" (1992, p. 204). We transform our language to present what we are saying in the way we wish to be understood. In other words, whatever we say (or write) is from a particular point of view and serves a particular purpose. This strategy is called 'spin' in the context of politics, and **gloss** in CA.

Goffman (1959), like Shakespeare, recognised that we have a repertoire of different roles that we play, according to whom we are speaking. The role we adopt depends on how we see ourselves and how we see others in the context of what we are trying to do and where we stand in regard to the particular stage of a relationship. Role-playing depends on how each individual perceives the role. Moreover, that perception changes as the relationship develops. When I was a mother with small children, my view of myself in that role was governed by the knowledge that I had to take responsibility for them from the beginning of their lives. Hutchby (1999) opines that both participants in **talk-in-interaction** continuously change their roles through the demands of the unfolding dialogue. This process is called mutual ratification.

As a young mother, I discovered that my role was continuously changing through my adaptation to my children's developing needs. The transition from helpless babyhood to independent adulthood is such a gradual process that it is easy to miss some of the cues and give our children either too much help or too little. They need our ongoing support but the nature of this support changes as they become responsible for themselves. In a healthy family the supervisory role gradually lessens and fades away.

Being fortunate enough to have children with whom I have a lot in common makes it easy to talk to them as equals and friends. Nevertheless, they are my children and I want to see them make the most of their lives. I can never entirely relinquish feelings of anxiety when things go wrong for them and joy when all is well, because I shall always feel they are a part of myself (as indeed they once were before they were born), and what affects them affects me. This factor is not entirely missing with unrelated friends, but too much of it would be obtrusive. No-one wants to feel s-mothered by another.

In psychotherapy my own experience as a parent has been invaluable. Clients need both support and respect for their independence. Getting the balance right is not easy, as every client is different. Ongoing experience, when its lessons are learned and digested by practitioners, helps us to improve the quality of our work.

We cannot speak to each other without revealing our sense of 'who we are'. If we have a realistic self-image we are less likely to feel the need to talk about ourselves. If our sense of well-being is based on an unrealistic self-image, we have a greater motive to defend ourselves from discovering the real state of play. If we are busy defending ourselves from being seen in a different way from how we wish to be seen, we are handicapped from engaging in free and spontaneous communication because we feel constrained to focus on ourselves and not on the person with whom we are talking (see Chapter Four).

The less we worry about how we are perceived by others the more we convey a sense of being at ease with ourselves. This is the foundation for the building of rapport.

(d) How we categorise others

Whenever we meet people for the first time, we categorise them in one way or another so that we can have some kind of idea of how to speak to them. That is why it is easier to talk to strangers if we meet them in a particular context, for example, a seminar for professionals or in a business setting where we have a particular task to fulfil. We already know something about what we have in common.

If we have no clues of this kind we are thrown back on our personal experience of interchanges with other people that go right back to the earliest times in our lives. We all carry with us a selection of stereotypes that we have constructed for ourselves based on our experience of encounters with others. We make use of these preformed categorisations as a guide to how we behave and talk with an unknown person. Sacks' names this resource the **MCD**, short for **Membership Categorisation Device** (1992).

In CA membership has a particular meaning connected with categorisation. There are many different types of categories, and everyone's way of defining them depends on their personal experience including their ability to make connections, as we saw above in the story of my son's use of 'iggle-iggle'. There are sets of categories and each set classifies a population. A population is a group of people or objects that have something in common.

The following is a schema showing the categories of human beings where the scope of the categories varies from very big to very small.

Populations	Scope
All human beings	Maximum
All adult human beings	↑
All child human beings	
All human beings who are university professors	↓
All human beings who are over 100 years old	Minimum

These are short cut ways of looking at groups of people. The bigger the scope the greater the generalisation. When we say things like "What do women want?" or "You know what men are like", we all know that both these utterances are likely to be complaints. We know that these utterances come from the frustrations of men and women failing to understand each other. The underlying assumptions are that it is feasible that all women want the same thing, and that all men have the same set of characteristics. The greater the scope of the generalisation the greater the distortion.

When we look at the category with the smallest scope, we are far more likely to come up with assumptions that could be true for most of that population. We know that most people aged 100 or more would be unlikely to run in a marathon and likely to die soon. The narrower the scope of the generalisation, the lesser the distortion.

Yet Sacks concluded that one of the extraordinary aspects of ordinary conversation is that **generalisations** are very rarely challenged. This has to do with a major difference between ordinary conversation and therapeutic talk. Jefferson and Lee (1992) noticed some differences between how **troubles-telling** is responded to in ordinary conversation and in a service-providing context, such as counselling. In ordinary conversation, troubles-tellers expect emotional reciprocity, that is, a sympathetic response, and in a professional situation, like psychotherapy, they expect to receive help and/or advice. When professionals try to 'humanise' their responses, difficulties can arise because they set about it in an inappropriate way. The authors suggest that an alternative could be for professionals to "recognise and enhance the deeply remedial potential of emotional reciprocity." (Jefferson and Lee, 1992, p. 521–548)

In Part Two of this book I shall show how therapists can maintain emotional reciprocity and at the same time remain focused on a neutral and unbiased pursuit of the roots of a client's problem which includes the challenging of generalisations and the unpacking of their meaning by the person using them. I shall now return to the question of why we need to have a shared, commonly accepted view of the world to be able to talk together in everyday conversation.

Economy in conversation

We are able to talk to many different kinds of people and maintain a coherent conversation. We can do this because we have a short cut system that almost everyone understands. We are usefully lazy in that we find the easiest and quickest route to the accomplishment of all actions, whether we are driving to a destination, building a house, using a computer or carrying out a social action through conversation.

Paradoxically, in order to find the easiest route, we have to go through a period of learning that can be complex and frustrating. I am in the middle of this process at the minute since I have bought a new kind of computer. I am just beginning to feel more confident as I use it, but for the first month I was continually frustrated, making so many mistakes that I often wondered if I had done the right thing. However the sense of achievement as I improve every day is highly pleasurable. I am beginning to find the short cuts through my greater understanding of the underlying principles.

Of course we do not know how our ancestors managed to get to the short cut stage when they were learning the new skill of speech. I imagine it must have been a matter of trial and error that went on for a long time and caused all sorts of difficulties. We need to remember that language is in a constant state of change. This has advantages and disadvantages. For example, although I can speak and read French well, I have not spoken it for many years. I have been obliged to buy a set of cassettes to bring me up to date with modern idioms.

The demands of the social task of psychotherapy

(a) The need for security and the need to make changes

A fundamental purpose for effective psychotherapy is to help clients to get a balance between maintaining a sense of security and being willing to take risks. There is a fundamental conflict between our need for security and our desire for excitement and adventure. When we are young and dependent on others we need to feel secure. We prefer the status quo. All those who are involved in child-rearing know how children thrive best in a structured daily routine, and will get very upset if a favourite toy or comfort blanket goes missing.

Yet alongside this yearning for sameness, infant humans are in an ongoing state of physiological and mental change which urges them to explore the new environment into which they are born. The natural progression from babyhood to adulthood moves away from dependence and towards independence to a greater or lesser degree related to the inherent nature of individuals and the influences of their upbringing. This process depends on our managing to get a balance between trying to be too safe and taking too many risks. This is illustrated by the following spectrum:

Safety _____ Danger

Paradoxically, to live at either end of this spectrum is dangerous. Having always worked for myself, apart from five years of teaching in schools, I am often asked by clients what it takes to be self-employed. One of the most pervasive questions is "How can I be sure that I will not lose money?" The only possible answer is we cannot be sure, either of that or of anything else. Taking risks is an essential part of living one's life, not just drifting through it and reacting passively to external events. I ask such clients to consider when are the only two times that we are guaranteed absolute safety. The answer is before we are conceived and after we are dead. All people who work for themselves risk losing everything. The most successful have nearly always got into severe financial problems at least once in their careers.[4]

The main reason for the popularity of psychotherapy is that many people are not independent enough and need some help in understanding why this should be so and what they can do to alter the situation. This includes the recognition that we must find a balance between feeling secure and being willing to try new things.

The growth and development of human beings requires that once we have mastered a new skill and got used to it, we look for a fresh challenge. However, learning is something we have to learn how to do. Yet I have never seen it as a subject on a school curriculum. It is a gradual, empirical process most of the time and we have to work it out for ourselves. Nothing is easy at first, and we all tend to take the easiest path if we can. Motivation can only come from inside ourselves. Having a good reason for doing something is imperative. If we want something enough we will be able to tolerate the frustration and disappointment and intermittent dissatisfaction that is an inevitable part of the creative process of learning new things and making changes.

Establishing relationships with each other depends on how we talk together. It is because we use economy in conversation through generalisation, deletion and distortion that we are able to understand each other. The distortions that arise from generalisations and deletions heighten the incidence of ambiguity and are a frequent cause of misunderstanding. Sacks himself recognised that what makes conversation possible is the very thing that causes difficulties in mutual understanding.

As I have described above, in order to understand the world we need to categorise the objects around us, ourselves, and each other. All categorisations are short cuts and involve generalisations, deletions and distortions. If they did not, every time we tried to describe anything, we should get lost in the effort to portray every aspect of what we are describing. We all know people who rarely finish a story because they are trying to do that very thing. They go off at tangents and forget the thread of their main talk in their efforts to get every detail right. Whether we are writing or speaking, clarity is the result of being able to prioritise what is relevant to what we are doing. What we leave out is as important as what we leave in.

(b) Proverbs, myths and legends, fables and other formulaic elements

Proverbs, myths and legends are an important part of our heritage. After people had learned to use speech and before they had learned to write, they told stories to each other to try and understand the world they lived in and the nature of human beings. An oral tradition of story-telling developed that formed the basis of an empirical understanding of the world. Carl Gustav Jung travelled all over the world visiting remote tribes and collecting details about their traditional myths and legends. His great discovery was that, although these ancient civilisations were separated by time and space, the stories they told had a great deal in common. The same characters emerged again and again.

Jung claimed that all religious systems contained a hierarchy of different gods, each one of whom had powers to oversee certain aspects of nature and human nature. All systems contained a heaven and an underworld. All gods required to be worshipped and to be offered sacrifices. All gods reflected human beings' ideas about themselves. Each god had individual characteristics that revealed what people observed in themselves and others. They were capable of all kinds of human feelings and responses: love, anger, spite, jealousy, revenge and mercy. They were capricious and unpredictable. Failure to worship and sacrifice would incur their wrath and bring down punishments on the offender.

Jung (1959) codified these characters that appeared not only in religious systems but also in fairy tales and called them archetypes. Each archetype stood for one aspect of human nature. He was then able to develop his own work, which was based initially on that of Freud, by using his discovery to understand how these different archetypes exist in all human beings, constituting a strong influence on their behaviour.[5]

Fables, moral tales whose purpose was to teach children how and how not to behave, are inhabited by animals who have human characteristics, being able to talk and act as people do. Like the hierarchy of gods, where each god represents one aspect of human behaviour there exists a hierarchy in the animal kingdom. For example, foxes are 'sly' and 'devious', lions are 'brave'.

Fairy tales follow the same pattern, but mainly have a cast of human beings. The supernatural element is also present in the form of fairy godmothers, but not fairy godfathers, witches who turn princes into frogs and put spells on infant princesses, wise old women, but few wise old men, and helpful, speaking animals. They are full of stock characters, kings and queens, wicked stepmothers (but interestingly enough, stepfathers rarely feature. When they do, they are usually depicted as being led by the nose by their wives), ugly ducklings growing into swans, despised and ill-treated youngest sons and daughters who have to overcome difficulties through suffering and hard work but always get their reward in the end. A characteristic of most folklore is the implication that good overcomes evil in the long run. Whilst we know that this is not always so, most of us like to believe this is true. Psychologically it is better for us to live hopefully.

The oral story-telling tradition reveals the way that people of all nations at all times categorise human nature, which forms part of a large body of common knowledge based on universal observations that all people of all kinds can understand. We need to remember that it was a long time in human history before the knowledge of different aspects of the world began to be studied as separate sciences. Aristotle is noted for his work in identifying different sciences and giving them names. This speeded up the move away from common-sense knowledge towards an academic approach.

Yet, all academic knowledge originates in somebody noticing something and asking a question. We still learn from observation, without having to be taught. This kind of learning has its own value and is the foundation of our belief systems about how the world works. It is based on our inheritance from myths, legends and fairy tales and strengthened by our own individual life experiences.

We all bring to our discourse with other people, not only academic, learned knowledge, but also our own view of the world which, although it is unique to us, contains many common elements that everyone in our particular environment, knows. They are manifested through the way we talk to each other, especially in our own particular environment, and our shared knowledge of **formulaic language**. Such language is so familiar to us that we do not question its meaning. The two most prevalent groups in this category are **proverbs** and oft-repeated generalisations.

Sacks (1992) was fascinated by proverbs . Like poetry, they say a lot in a few words and are easy to remember because of the rhythm and cadence of their structure. They are not axiomatic statements of absolute truths. They are metaphors that are 'correct about something'. They are not logical propositions that can be proved true or false. Sacks points out that people do not expect to be questioned about the truth of a proverb, and they do not like it if they are. Such formulaic elements constitute short cuts to meaning in conversation because they are widely known and accepted and people can interpret them as they wish because they are metaphors and can be adapted to a variety of situations.

There are proverbs that appear to be contradictory. For example, many hands make light work, and too many cooks spoil the broth. Yet we can clearly see that both could be right in different contexts. Six people weed a garden quicker than one, provided they can all recognise a weed when they see it. Yet the making of broth depends on one person who knows what is going on. If other people interfere with the process it may well go wrong.

Formulaic phrases are different. They are not traditional, yet when they are constantly used they develop a power of their own which can cause difficulties in conversation. A familiar one that crops up in psychotherapy when I am working with marital problems is 'you know what men (or women) are like don't you?' In everyday talk it is very difficult to challenge this generalisation without breaking rapport, because what the speaker is really doing here is trying to get the recipient to agree with a prejudice. Giving support to a troubled person differs from colluding with them. The exigencies of psychotherapy require that this kind of generalisation be challenged.

This vast body of folklore and formulaic phrases makes it possible for very different people to talk together and understand each other at a basic level. Thus it is of great importance in facilitating economy in conversation.

The practicalities of psychotherapy practice

Psychotherapy, like all professional services, is time limited. The standard duration of a one-to-one consultation is fifty minutes. As a working therapist, although I do not always adhere rigidly to this rule, I find the constraint of time helpful, in as much as it obliges me to maintain a balance between not putting undue pressure to respond on the client and bearing in mind the importance of **relevance**. Short cuts in therapy talk are essential, but they need to be skilfully employed in order not to put undue pressure on clients.

Clients are inevitably looking for therapists with whom they can feel comfortable enough to talk about those matters that cause them pain. A vital aspect is therapists' ability to create and maintain a feeling of rapport with clients. The components of rapport required from therapists are:

a) A genuine interest in clients' lives and difficulties.
b) Careful listening including giving responses that give appropriate feed-back and encouragement.
c) The ability to decide what kind of **interventions** to make and when. This includes the monitoring of what is and is not relevant.
d) Knowing the difference between neutral **alignment** (sticking to the main topic) and emotional **affiliation** (demonstrations of empathy) and knowing how to use them appropriately.

(a) is essential, and has best been described by Rogers (1957) as unconditional positive regard. As therapists we need to remember that we are human beings, who do not have unlimited reserves of patience and understanding. Whenever two people talk together they inevitably influence each other. Freud (1940) calls this process transference and counter transference. In everyday language this means that how two people respond to each other is affected by all their previous experiences, especially early family relationships (see next chapter).

Stereotypical ideas about what people are like get in the way of mutual understanding. For example, since many of my clients are of an age similar to my own children's, talking to me can remind them of how they felt about their real mothers. This causes a distortion in how they see me as a unique individual. By the same token, I can do the same thing in reverse.

The management of this situation depends on the skills of therapists, who need two useful resources. First, the ability to maintain ongoing attention to their own cognitive and emotional processes, so that they can recognise the difference between feelings that arise from their own previous experiences and those that represent a genuine response to clients. Second to use the same process in order to decipher the meaning of clients' inappropriate responses. This ability to make neutral assessments of a situation is an essential for the avoidance of getting into arguments with clients, which can be disastrous for the maintenance of rapport.

This does not mean therapists have to collude with clients by accepting statements that reveal an unhelpful attitude or belief. It means that we must be very careful in how we handle such a situation. This is one of the reasons why I believe that the practice of psychotherapy is an art rather than a science, as I maintained earlier.

Points (b), (c), and (d) all follow on from (a), and will be discussed and illustrated with extracts from live therapy talk taken from my PhD data in Part Two of this book.

(a) The need for relevance

Many clients come to therapy with the belief that the main purpose is to unburden themselves. True, this is a part of the process. However, one of the reasons that people do not value psychotherapy is because they think it is no better than talking to a friend.[6] In fact it is very different, as I hope to make clear in this book. One of the main differences is that clients are not encouraged to complain at length, which is what usually happens when they talk to friends. They are encouraged to understand that complaining is a passive activity that will not help them to solve their problem because they are looking outside themselves for a solution, instead of recognising that it is inner scrutiny that gets results.

One could spend hours listening to them as I know from earlier experience before I did my training. It is true that people may feel better afterwards, but it will not last long and they may well have reinforced their sense of grievance through talking about it too much.[7] They are not usually looking for help but agreement and sympathy. Neither of these responses helps them to find a solution to their problem. Moreover, friends do not have the necessary knowledge and training to know how to deal with the situation.

One of the essentials of therapy talk is to stay with the main topic, which is the diagnosis, prognosis and treatment of clients' problems. Therapists' first task is to get clients to talk (see Chapter Five). Once clients have begun a troubles-telling, therapists can begin to collect clues from the way they tell it (see Chapter 6). The actual content of the **troubles-telling** is irrelevant. It is merely a vehicle from which therapists collect information that relates to the underlying topic, the clients' problem.

(b) Talking to topic

The notion of topic is related to the subject of categorisation. Sacks gives an example from a telephone conversation where the caller wants to rent a house:

> "A: When can we see it.
> B: I'll tell you, uh the woman who lives there now, uh will be there for a while, and I haven't arranged with her yet to show it." (Sacks, 1992, p. 752)

Note that 'the woman who lives there now' is a special way of categorising, or characterising, to use Sacks' term, this particular woman. As Sacks comments, when you know that the conversation is about someone wanting to rent a house, the reason for this characterisation is obvious. B's response to A's request to see the house is an explanation about why B cannot do so at once. Thus the topic is not about someone wanting to rent a house. It is about why there is a delay in A being able to see it.

This is clarified by B's reply that there is a woman living in it and permission to see it has to be required first from her. Her characterisation as a tenant leads to B's understanding that he cannot see the house straight away. The characterisation of persons is a technique that draws attention to the topic in hand. Sacks points out that this is only one of a number of devices that serve as clues to the identification of the topic.

In Chapter 6, there is an example of the therapist trying to identify the underlying topic of a troubles-telling. In therapy, the constraint of time makes it essential that irrelevant material is discarded as soon as possible. This does not happen in ordinary conversation.

(c) The flexibility of lexical items

We have already said something about the ambiguity of words (see Chapter One). Ferdinand de Saussure defined words as signs standing for an object. Wittgenstein (1953) and Sacks (1992) discussed the importance of the effect of context on the meaning of words. The understanding of the context in which talk takes place enables us to understand the meaning of the words used in that context. The flexibility of the meaning of words leads to a great economy in the number of different words we need to know. However, there is a downside to this. It increases the opportunities for misunderstandings. To reiterate, as Sacks said, the very thing that makes the conduct of conversation possible is a cause of misunderstandings.

The next chapter is concerned with how we make sense of the world and are able to communicate with each other because of this ability to categorise, another short cut essential for the understanding of the process of conversation.

Conclusion

In this chapter I have attempted to pull together the components of some of those short cuts that make intelligible talk possible. I hope to have said enough about the practice of psychotherapy so far to show that short cuts are also necessary in maintaining **relevance** to the pursuit of the diagnosis and possible solution of the client's problem. My list is by no means exhaustive. I have selected those aspects of short cuts that are relevant to the book.

Of course we are not consciously aware of what we are doing. Readers might ask: If we already know how to do it why should we bother to learn the underlying structure? This is the same kind of question as: If we can talk without learning grammar, why should we bother to learn it? The answer is simple. Once we understand how something is done it is easier to see how we can improve it. We do not need to understand how a car works in order to be able to drive. But some knowledge of how cars work can give us insight into how we could recognise certain symptoms that are evidence that some part of the machine is not working. Greater knowledge can also lead to improved driving skills.

By the same token psychological studies throw considerable light on the dynamics of underlying beliefs and subsequent behaviour. The study of body language and physiological and emotional symptoms goes some way towards explaining difficulties in communication. But until the advent of Harvey Sacks, no-one understood the underlying components that enable talk-in-interaction to work as it does.

The first three chapters have provided background material for the understanding of Chapter Four, the most important factor for effective psychotherapy, the therapeutic relationship. There are still some therapists that do not accept this idea, but there is a powerful and ever-growing movement towards the recognition of the importance of this premise.

NOTES

1. A study of how children categorise can help us to understand their potential interests. I believe this theme is worthy of a new research project. We can learn about how their mind works by examining how they do it.

2. This example explains why the basic level category is the first we learn. Until we have grasped that, we cannot understand either finer detail or wider groups. Our minds have to learn to be more aware of differences: a gradual process that depends on the development of the brain.

3. There has always been a strong resistance to the acceptance that human beings are part of the animal kingdom. This is reflected, like everything else, in how we use language. The formulaic term 'he behaved like an animal' is certainly not meant as a compliment. The truth is that because the behaviour of animals (in wild surroundings) consists of their instinctive responses to the imperatives of the basic needs for survival and reproduction, they have not had the opportunity to develop some of the nastier aspects of human beings, such as killing for no good reason. However, the work of Darwin, and the development of evolutionary psychology has gone a long way to counteracting this idea. Much has been written about the superiority of humans to animals because of our larger, more sophisticated brains and our language ability. Yet, as many writers have shown, the growth of civilisation has not always improved human behaviour.

4. Contrary to what we might expect from the contents of some self-help books, it is not enough to have an optimistic outlook. Two of my most successful clients have made it clear that had they not gone into all the things that could go wrong in a new venture before they had committed themselves, they might not have succeeded. Thus there is a big difference between a calculated risk and an uncalculated one.

5. Jung's theory of archetypes constitutes part of his wider theory of the universal unconscious.

6. This is the reason why the vernacular title of my PhD thesis, and this book, is *Not Just Talking*. I am weary of the constantly reiterated misapprehension that psychotherapy is 'just talking' and can

be carried out by a friend. This not only fails to acknowledge the body of psychological knowledge about human dynamics, and by so doing, debases the profession, but it also undervalues the skills involved in conversation itself.

7. There is a common feeling that talking too much about our troubles tends to reinforce them and that therefore people should forget about them and get on with their lives. There is some truth in this, which is why troubles-telling in therapy is regarded more as a source for clues to the client's problem rather than for the actual content of their stories. A good therapist does not need to hear many stories about the same topic, which makes this process very different from what happens in everyday conversation when people talk of their miseries to exact sympathy from others. Sympathy does not resolve problems nor does it help people to work things out for themselves.

CHAPTER FOUR

The therapeutic relationship

A
lthough the importance of the relationship between therapist and client was first tacitly recognised by Freud, in his formulation of the transference/counter transference, and by Jung, through his recognition that the process of psychotherapy changes both therapist and client it was not until Carl Rogers (1957) developed his method of client-centred therapy that serious attention was given to the analysis of this relationship as an essential part of the therapeutic task.

Although the meaning of the term therapeutic relationship was coined to describe what goes on between therapists and clients, one of the chief aims in this book is to show that what I learned through my PhD research about the structure of the dialogue in psychotherapy, can be usefully applied to all speech-exchange systems where the emphasis is on cooperation for mutual benefit. Therefore I use the term in a wider sense. This chapter explores the basic structure of human development and adjustment to the world that both makes conversation possible and imposes necessary constraints upon it.

Before Sacks, conversation was taken for granted as something that everyone can do. The complexity of how we manage to understand each other through talk-in-interaction had gone totally unrecognised. Words are codes, and the meanings attributed to them can be ambivalent since they depend on three factors, first, who is saying them, second, who is listening to them and third the context in which the talk takes place. Yet at the same time, there is a body of common knowledge about meanings that we all understand, for example, that a dog is a dog, and a rose is a rose, and a dog rose is a dog rose.

In the last chapter I discussed how we make our own categorisations of the animate and inanimate world around us. When we share the same culture and background there will be similarities in our generalised understandings. Each group of people living and working together establishes a mini-culture of their own, and develops its own private use of language that may not be easily accessible to outsiders. Clubs of all kinds and special interest groups provide for us a place where we can be sure of finding others with whom we know we shall have something in common. The attraction of such groups is their exclusivity, which is enhanced by special kinds of clothes, for example old school ties, and other specific signs that enable us to recognise fellow **members**, even when we have not seen them before.

Clients who embark on a course of psychotherapy become part of a special group that develops a different kind of personal interaction from ordinary conversation. They learn how therapy talk is done through the dialogue with their therapists. Wittgenstein (1953) described all activities, verbal or otherwise, as games that have their own rules. Psychotherapy is a game played by two: a self-developing creative activity that takes place under the guidance of a professional, whose skills are used to help others to discover more about themselves. The process involves changes in attitudes and beliefs, which are brought into being through a reorganisation of thinking and speaking. The basis of many different psychotherapeutic models is the theory that we absorb beliefs and patterns of behaviour in the first few years of life through a process of osmosis, which provides us with a model as a starting point to help us to develop our personal model of the world and our relationship to it.

There is a major drawback to this process. Before our minds have developed sufficiently for us to be able to question this model, we are already imbued with a template for living of which we are unaware at a conscious level. Inevitably this model for living is imperfect, because each individual has different inherited characteristics and has different needs. The maturation process involves conscious and unconscious processes working together, through a process of trial and error, to enable us to survive.

Survival involves finding occupations to earn enough money, and discovering activities to fill our leisure time. How we set about doing this depends on the kind of people we are. This necessitates our finding a place on the following spectrum:

Passive ———————————————————————— Active

At one extreme we can allow ourselves to accept the environment we are born into by going with the flow. At the other extreme, we can choose to use our powers of thinking to challenge the environment by making an effort to change it. Most people tend to remain close to the passive end of the spectrum, because it is easier to stay with what is known than to face the risks of the unknown. The snag is that if we are too passive our lives can be warped by our reluctance to remove ourselves from an unsatisfactory environment and to change the way we do things. The maxim 'an unconsidered life is an unlived life' makes the point that if we make no effort to change ourselves then we cannot expect anything other than having to put up with whatever happens to us. The result of such an attitude is that we place far too much faith in the belief that something will turn up out of the blue and solve our problems. This accounts for the popularity of lotteries for example.

Active people make plans in the belief that they can increase the possibility of good fortune. They do not expect luck to come to them, they make things happen by spotting new opportunities and trying them out. If they are fundamentally benevolent, they may become involved in an ongoing struggle to understand themselves in order to find ways to make use of their natural resources for the benefit of themselves and others. This process inevitably involves two factors, an ability to deal with their own inner conflicts, and the courage to make decisions. Such people lead more conscious lives, because they *want* to be more aware of what they are doing.

Human beings have become far more conscious of themselves since they developed the power of speech. Once we can put thoughts and feelings into words we begin to use logic and argument to challenge our unconscious assumptions and those of the society into which we have been born. However, because we all have beliefs and patterns of behaviour that we do not know we have, we cannot think in a purely rational way as Bertrand Russell (1990) realised. The main handicap is the template that we have absorbed and which remains unconscious unless we make a determined effort to understand it. A major part of psychotherapy consists of the task of understanding conflicts, rather than working at a superficial level by trying directly to 'cure' symptoms.[1] We cannot change anything until we understand the underlying nature of the problem.

Early unconscious learning taken in from the environment has a powerful effect on our belief systems. The very fact that this learning is intertwined with our needs for security and a sense of belonging in society reinforces our feelings of 'rightness' about what we were taught. The result is a state of conflict between unconscious beliefs and our need to think things through for ourselves.

Whilst we cannot avoid physical changes that occur naturally as we grow older, the ageing process in itself does not lead to wisdom. When we are born we are unconscious of who we are and what is going on around us. Awareness evolves gradually throughout life or it may never evolve. There are people whose level of unquestioning acceptance of their circumstances ensures that they remain as unconscious at seventy as they were at seven, hence the maxim 'there's no fool like an old fool'. The step from accepting everything in our environment to beginning to question what we want to take in and what we would rather leave out requires active thought.

Before we can begin to look at what happens when two people talk together, we must first understand how human beings develop a particular view of their own lives and the world about them. I have already described some of the purposes of conversation in Chapter Two and the way we categorise objects and people in Chapter Three. I shall now consider how human beings progress from birth to adulthood in the following schema. The explication of this schema will put us into a position that will clarify the resources that are available to us when we participate in spontaneous conversation. I shall analyse the following themes in order:

• The explication of the schema
• Intrasubjectivity and intersubjectivity

A model showing stages of the dynamics of change in the evolution of a human being

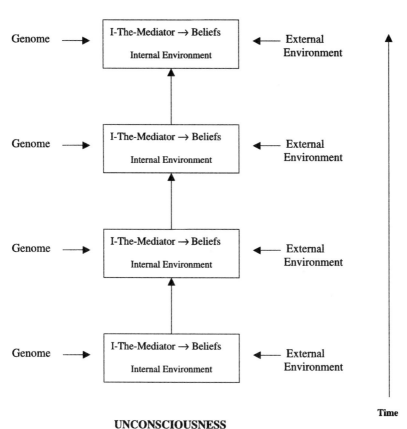

CONSCIOUSNESS

UNCONSCIOUSNESS

Key

The Genome embodies all our inherited characteristics: the building blocks of human development

I-The-Mediator is the self that processes the interaction between the genome and the external environment in order to construct knowledge and beliefs

Internal Environment includes inner stages of thinking and feeling

External Environment comprises both the animate and inanimate world around us

The activities of the genome are basically twofold. First: "Every organism possesses a genome that contains the biological information needed to construct and maintain a living example of that organism" (Brown, 1999, p. 2). Our physiological growth is largely outside our control. It is an unconscious process that is managed by the autonomous nervous system. However, we are not entirely without power to help our biological growth to flourish as it should. We can eat foods that are good for us, avoid taking in what is not good for us, and make sure that we develop our muscles and bones to their maximum potential by taking exercise.

Second, our particular genes and the way they combine with each other in many different ways, comprise the raw material of our emotions and our skills. We become aware of our temperament and what attracts and repels us in the outside world through our ongoing exposure to it. How we perceive our external environment constantly brings to our attention aspects of the genome that have not been awakened.

I-The-Mediator is the term I use to define the totality of ourselves as conscious and unconscious beings. The environment, animate and inanimate objects in the outside world, is a variable and so is I-The-Mediator whose task is to recognize and interpret the connection between the external environment and its effect on the genome and vice versa. This is an internal process that psychologists call **intrasubjectivity**. It is related to the state of internal dialogue that I discussed in Chapter Two.

Our unconscious minds include the way our genes work for us to keep our bodies in working order and the effect that our inherited characteristics have on the sense we make of our internal and external environments. The genome is the blueprint that determines our biological growth and our inherited, individual characteristics. The genome is a constant, but we have to remember that cells do not faultlessly reproduce themselves all the time. They are subject to mutations. Nevertheless, the genome is stable enough to define our phenotype throughout our lives. Our physiology and biology are in an ongoing state of growth as cells are renewed and the myriad internal processes in our body chemistry are constantly changing, but the basic structure remains.

Whatever the nature and quality of our genetic inheritance, we cannot develop our potential without the help of the environment. We do not exist in a vacuum. We cannot develop our potential as individuals without an ongoing interaction with other people and with the external world within our own particular culture. Because we are all unique, there is no perfect environment for anyone.

This model starts off as an unconscious process. The internal environment is in a state of continuous change. We constantly study and renew our perceptions of the world through what we learn from our experience of it. I invite readers to see the four boxes as part of an indefinable number of different interpretations of both the internal and external worlds we live in. As we move away from the unconscious state in which we come into the world as babies we become more and more aware of the world around us. In theory, as we grow older, we develop a greater wisdom and understanding of ourselves, other people and the world we live in. But this does not necessarily happen. There is much truth in the adage 'there is no fool like an old fool'.

We all, to a greater or lesser degree, take what we have been taught for granted. Adults call this 'bringing children up' and 'teaching them right from wrong'. Fortunately for our development as individuals, many of us begin to question some of these ideas as our minds develop. However it is important not to throw out the baby with the bath water. Some of the constraints that are put upon us serve to keep us physically safe in the interests of ensuring that we reach adulthood. Teenage children have a marked tendency to rebel against constraints that irk them by refusing to accept those aspects of authority that they feel hold them back from developing as individuals.

The schema displays a pattern of learning that emerges as the ongoing effect of our role as I-The-Mediator comes to terms with the awakening of the potentials of our own particular genome through the influence of the external environment. For example if we have an innate talent for music, it cannot be aroused until we have first experienced hearing music from the external environment. What if we hear outside noises that awaken feelings of disgust or pain within us? We then become aware of something from the outside that appears to be a threat. Freud's theory of defence mechanisms explains the origins of such features as phobias, obsessive behaviour and psychosomatic symptoms as coping strategies which enable us to avoid the remembrance of painful feelings that we have buried years before in the depth of our unconscious mind. Once traumatic experiences have been unearthed and worked through, such symptoms can disappear like ice in fire.

The conscious and the unconscious mind

The schema shows that as we develop we move away from unconsciousness towards consciousness. Consciousness, that is, knowing that we exist and being able to make plans through time is a characteristics of humans. It does not happen in the animal kingdom, when animals are living in the wild and fending for themselves. They live largely unconscious lives.[2]

They are not aware of themselves as individuals except in a very primitive way. Their behaviour consists almost entirely of reactions to their basic needs to survive and preserve the species. They conform to the unwritten rules of their communities that have come into being through trial and error. It is easier to survive in groups than to be alone, although in the animal kingdom there are exceptions. Animals do not have the gift of speech as we know it. The massive growth of the neo-cortex was a necessary concomitant of the need to accommodate the development of language and all the new activities that speech has made possible.

All thinking is affected by four factors: first, our instincts/ emotions and senses, and second, our belief systems, the rules by which we lead our lives. Third, the capacity to speak has given us the power to translate our thoughts into words and fourth, the cognitive ability of our neo-cortex. This has led to a movement away from simplicity to complexity. We have powers to remember, to plan for the future, to be aware that we are alive and that we will die, and to learn to adapt ourselves to our environment or to change it if need be. We can acquire power over other peoples' lives. We can and do turn ourselves into living gods by achieving fame and recognition for both benevolent and malevolent actions.

This has made it possible for us to develop ideas not just in our own lifetime but to bequeath our discoveries to our descendants, so that they can build on it and develop it still further. Korzybski (1933) called this process time-binding:

> "What Korzybski fully recognised was the central, defining role of language. No language, no time-binding. If so then structures of languages must be determinative for time-binding." (Pula, 1994, p. xv)

As with all gifts, we pay a price for our excellent new brain. The more refined our ability to reason, the more we are capable of self-deception through the construction of spurious, but plausible arguments aimed to get us what we think we want. Those of us who live in a highly sophisticated society, far removed from the 'natural' environment of our distant ancestors, have learned to confuse 'needs' with 'wants'. This is a major source of our troubles. We have become imbued with the idea that if we get what we want we shall be happy. When we are not we feel short changed. We then work at getting more and more of what we think we want and then find we are getting less and less of what we need.

There is a long-standing debate about the meaning of consciousness. Velmans (2000) posits that being conscious means that we can observe phenomena and describe them with varying degrees of accuracy in ordinary language. Other people's experience might be 'hypothetical constructs' as we cannot observe their experiences in the direct way that we can observe or own. Velmans argues for the existence of a world of external objects that we can all recognise and respond to in a reflexive way, by reproducing a representation of the external image in our brain.

We all live in the same world and see the same things around us. What we make of them is a different matter, because the effect on our perceptions is not the same for everybody. We are conscious only of those objects that matter to us. This is the reason why witnesses of an accident or crime tell different stories. We all see the same event and respond to it differently. No-one notices everything, because that is not possible. The belief implied in the oath to 'tell the truth, the whole truth, and nothing but the truth' is fallacious because it is an impossibility. Each person can tell only the bit of truth that they have taken in and partial truths have a distorting effect on the whole picture.

The way we react to our experiences depends on the conclusions we have already come to about all the other experiences we have undergone from the beginning of our lives. This vast reservoir of information lies dormant in our unconscious mind for the simple reason that we can only focus on a limited number of objects at any one time in order to function at all. Everything else remains unconscious until we need it. If we unexpectedly meet someone we recognise, for the first time in many years, most of us take a while to remember that person's name. We may not recall it at all. There is a theory that we all remember, at some level, everything that has happened in our lives. However there is another theory that some memories become extinct because they are of little importance:

> "According to psychodynamics, relationships are driven by unconscious forces, many of which concern our use of other people, in our relationships, to satisfy needs which first surfaced in childhood and may have been repressed ever since." (Miell & Dallos, 1996, p. 158)

The idea of the unconscious mind and its effect on our lives was first crystallised into a concrete form by Freud (1957). This was not a new idea. The best literature in all nations recognises that we are driven by forces of which we are unaware. In "Macbeth", Shakespeare demonstrates how Lady Macbeth fails to understand herself well enough to imagine she could encourage the carrying out of an assassination without suffering severe trauma afterwards.

The implications of Freud's discovery were mind-blowing for me when I first began to read him at the age of eighteen. At last someone had given me some previously unimaginable tools that I had never encountered before. Everything I read made sense and filled me with hope that my powers to help myself were much greater than I had realised. I began to see that it was possible for me to begin to understand what I was doing that held me back, especially in my relationships with other people and in my studies. It is no mystery to me that so many people have felt the same. This accounts for the exponential development of psychotherapy over the last hundred and more years.

We are all affected, some if not all of the time, by unrecognised aspects of ourselves that overcome our powers of logical thought and realistic insight and lead us into actions that we bitterly regret, the result of motives we fail to understand. The only possible conclusion is that we have an enormous capacity to see only those arguments we want to see, and to hide from ourselves any possible unpleasant outcomes. This ability to sweep things under the carpet is what Freud called repression. We are so good at it that we can 'forget' whole sequences of our lives as a result, especially those that have caused us most pain. Freud used the term 'unconscious mind' to describe a repository that is not available, except under special circumstances, to our usual state of conscious awareness.

Common-sense tells us that we are far more likely to remember experiences linked with emotions. Happy times and distressing ones are likely to make a stronger impression on our bodies and minds. A study on the theme of accelerated learning (Rose, 1985) shows us how all learning is linked with emotions. For instance, if instruction, be it self-taught or learned from another, takes place in a pleasant environment students will not only learn in a more relaxed way but will retain what they have learned more clearly and for a longer period of time.

If we are forced to learn before we are ready to do so, in an atmosphere of coercion, we cannot fail to feel resentment and fear that if we do not learn we shall be punished. Since schools are compulsory, and classes are usually too big for teachers to be able to give that individual attention that is so important in teaching, many children who start off with a natural curiosity and desire to explore new things develop a resistance to study that is entirely understandable.[3] It is associated with negative feelings, and who wants to do anything that reminds them of feelings they would rather forget?

By the same token, if we have learned that to be in a family is an unhappy experience; the chances of our creating a better family of our own are reduced. We may either react negatively, by giving our spouse and/or children a hard time, or we can react positively and try to make up to them for our own suffering through being over-indulgent, lacking the capacity to allow our children to make their own mistakes. There is a third way. We can choose to rework and re-understand our own unrecognised beliefs through psychotherapy. A few people seem to be able to do this for themselves, but in my experience they are rare.

Many of our beliefs, attitudes and prejudices are absorbed unconsciously through our exposure to other people's opinions, especially in our earliest years when we are prone to accept what we are told because we have not yet had enough experience to be able to make our own judgements. However it would be a mistake to think that all children take everything on board. A new human being is naturally curious about the extraordinary world into which they are suddenly projected. Anyone who has had the experience of looking after babies knows that most of them take time to settle down into their new environment. Crying fits without any discernible reason are the norm for most babies. In their third year of life, most children go through the phase of rebellion and temper tantrums, which is so common that it has been given the name of 'the terrible twos'.

Becoming a parent is a difficult rite of passage because it is usually the first time in our lives when another human being is completely dependent on us. What is more the baby has no conception of time, and may not easily settle into a routine. Parents need great patience to help children to develop those **habits** that make their own lives easier and give a sense of security to the child. Any form of coercion will arouse resistance in a child of spirit. The more small children fight to get what they want, the more patience parents need to find ingenious ways of helping children to cope with their feelings of helplessness and anger, and at the same time manage their own.

When children do not feel that parents are in control, they feel unsafe and their behaviour becomes more extreme. Child care is such a difficult art that it is easy to see why so many of us are still trying to come to terms with childhood events decades after we have reached maturity. McLeod (2000) argues that we all need to make sense of our lives through bringing into awareness past events that have not been resolved in order to reconstruct them in a different way so that we can accept them and put them to rest. Only then shall we be free of the tyranny of the past over the present. In Chapter Seven there are examples of what I have called **retrospective reassessment**, the art of changing our attitude to painful memories by reconstructing them in a way that reveals how they have helped our personal development by giving us a greater understanding of ourselves and other people.

Intrasubjectivity and intersubjectivity

Intrasubjectivity

Steven Pinker (2002) has done much to raise awareness of the importance of our inherited characteristics, and, at the same time, he acknowledges the necessity for the stimulus of the environment for the development of inherited potential. It is the ongoing conflict between the demands of our genome, the driving force of our core self, and the external influences of people and society, that makes it necessary for us to be in a conscious state of trying to establish for ourselves a personal identity which will help us to make the best of our lives and at the same time to be able to make fruitful relationships with other people. This is the nature of the ongoing inner dialogue that I talked about in Chapter Two.

This process is called **intrasubjectivity** to distinguish it from **inter-subjectivity**, our ongoing dialogue with others. Whatever character traits we display through our own particular type of inner dialogue will affect our dialogue with others. If we are open with ourselves and try to be aware of all aspects of ourselves, including those we do not particularly like, the greater the possibility that we shall be more open in our dialogue with others. By the same token if we hide things from ourselves and allow ourselves to be governed by a false identity we have created for ourselves in order not to have to accept what we see as our shortcomings, we can be sure that our relationships with others will be less honest. We shall find it difficult to establish a beneficial and lasting relationship.

I have attempted to show how intrasubjectivity works in my schema. At every stage in life, I-The-Mediator has new work to do to adjust the self's understanding as it develops through the genome's response to outside influences. Language enables us to think with words about our sense of identity and what we want from life. We are more or less successful depending on where we fit on the passive/active spectrum. The more passive we are, the more we will take the easy way out and try to fit into the particular society we live in. The more active, the more likely we are to start to rebel against those aspects of society that we see as unhelpful by beginning to think for ourselves. Either way, I-The-Mediator will remain involved in an inner dialogue between the demands of our genome and outside pressures to conform. Wisdom grows out of the ability to distinguish what to change and what to leave alone. Too much change too quickly can have deleterious results. The Russian revolution is a good example where one repressive regime was replaced by another in the name of liberty.

Intersubjectivity

Miel & Dallos have defined intersubjectivity as "the sense of connectedness, similarity of experience, understanding of and empathy with another person." (Miel & Dallos 1996, p. 102) Sacks made a major contribution to the understanding of intersubjectivity through his ground-breaking recognition of the importance of conversation as the result of people talking together to arrive as close as they could to mutual understanding: a new domain in its own right that offered unlimited possibilities for the improvement of human cooperation.

Every time we talk with another person, each of us demonstrates, rarely realising exactly what we are doing, how we feel about ourselves, what we believe, how we see other people and the strength or weakness of our emotions. All this is conveyed through the way we use language and paralinguistic behaviour. People who are good at influencing others, and skilful in managing personal interactions are usually well above the average in picking up these clues and interpreting them correctly. The words we use to describe this gift are empathy and rapport. In psychotherapy, the responsibility for the provision of these essentials for the establishment of an environment of trust lies with the therapist.

The therapeutic relationship

As a result of my life experience and my professional training I believe that the quality of the relationship between therapist and client depends on the following factors:

- The degree of self-knowledge and professional expertise of the therapist.
- The degree of self-knowledge of the client.
- The ability of the therapist to establish a secure environment for the client through gaining the client's trust.
- The strength of the client's motivation to overcome personal difficulties that get in the way of making changes.
- The open-mindedness of both participants and the willingness of both to share experiences that could be helpful with each other.
- The therapist's sense of timing, when making **interventions**, is of the utmost importance. Therapists who listen attentively and give appropriate feedback and at the same time maintain rapport, will usually be able to gauge what to say and when.

There are good arguments for the belief that whatever problems clients bring to therapists, whatever the physiological manifestations that appear to be inaccessible to medical intervention, are the results of inner conflicts between unconscious and conscious forces.

The aim of psychotherapy is to help clients to become aware of unconscious motives and beliefs that affect their patterns of behaviour, by bringing them into consciousness in order to understand them better. This awareness enables them to begin to take charge of their lives in a way that makes the fullest possible use of their resources for the benefit of their lives.

When two people engage in dialogue, they are communicating on two levels, the conscious and the unconscious. How we understand each other's utterances is based on everything we have learned about life and other people. We all have our own ideas about the meaning of the words we use and the way we use them. As Sacks has shown us, all conversation is full of **repairs**. We are constantly correcting our own utterances and those of other people in the effort to understand each other. It is a wonder that we can achieve any kind of meaningful communication, apart from phatic talk. Once we have grasped this fully, it is easy to see how misunderstandings can arise so easily and so frequently.

Each participant's use of their personal intrasubjectivity affects the kind and quality of their intersubjectivity with others. Self-understanding is quintessential for the understanding of others.

Power and psychotherapy

Therapists are entrusted with enormous power by their clients. It is of the utmost importance that they know how to use it well and not for their own self-aggrandisement. I aim to show the importance of cooperation in the active pursuit by both participants of the source of the client's problems. In Chapters Five, Six and Seven, which comprise the main body of my PhD findings, my focus is on the analysis of how a new kind of cooperative dialogue evolves that makes use of the resources of both participants. Diagnosis, the unravelling of the origin of clients' disaffection with their lives, evolves as a result of joint participation.

Each of us is a unique individual, with our own innate potential. This may seem like an obvious statement, but the fact is that, when we pay attention to what is going on around us every day, we begin to realise that people not only expect others to be like themselves but even worse, they treat them as though they *were*. One of the most crippling aspects of this attitude is the belief that we know what is best for our children. It is true that we know the physical needs of helpless human beings during the earliest period after birth and rightly pay attention to them. However, individual differences begin to manifest themselves very soon.

Giving advice gratuitously, offering to help inappropriately (the do-gooder syndrome), telling other people what they ought to do, are but a few examples of the attempt to control others. Why should we want to do this? If we are happy with the way we are, and manage our lives realistically, what pleasure can we possibly get through trying to interfere in others' lives? Well, Freud told us it all begins in childhood and he was right.

A new phrase has crept into our vocabulary over the last fifty years. It is 'the selfish society'[4]. It is often used to imply that psychotherapy is a self-indulgent activity. In fact it is an exercise that requires us to take responsibility for ourselves by getting to know ourselves better. It is no easy matter to embark on the search to understand ourselves, warts and all. Once we begin to do this, we become more tolerant of others' 'failings' and more skilled in our relationships. Self-understanding leads to a rejection of self-righteousness and more respect for others.

Respect is the key word we need to remember, the one that is most helpful in avoiding the improper use of power. If we respect other people's individuality, their point of view; their differences and yet can still disagree without getting into a violent argument and indulging in character assassination, we have take the first steps towards real cooperation.

Our sense of personal identity

There are two kinds of identity, group and personal. Before our ancestors learned to speak, group identity was the most important. A group of people could pool their resources and provide a safe environment for rearing their young and fighting off predators, both wild animals and other tribes. Every individual played a part in contributing to the welfare of all. Everyone knew what was expected from them. The battle to survive took up a lot of energy, and time left over was spent in resting, sleeping and playing.

Since then groups have grown larger and larger and become far more complex. It is more difficult for individuals to find a group into which they can comfortably fit, giving them a sense of belonging and of being valued for their own contribution to the general good.

Confusion about how to live one's life causes anxiety and insecurity. One of the signs of our particular zeitgeist is the emphasis that we put on individual identity. A common reason for seeking therapy is people's need to understand themselves and what they 'really want to do'.

Until the middle of the twentieth century, the vast majority of people did not have the time or opportunity for such worries. In western nations, with no welfare state and severe economic problems, it was enough if people had a job of any kind so that they could keep themselves and their families housed, fed and clothed. Men worked long hours in tedious and often dangerous jobs. Without labour-saving devices wives and mothers were so exhausted that there was no time nor reason to worry if they were making the most of their lives. We can only allow ourselves such luxuries when we are not continually anxious about being out of work and going hungry.

Ironically, it is the increased recognition of people's rights to get help when they are out of work through no fault of their own, and their rights to proper medical care whether they can afford it or not, that has given people the space to realise how unsatisfactory many of their lives are. The things that make life easier give us the time to ask ourselves what our lives are for.

Conclusion

This chapter is about how we manage to talk together in a way that engenders friendliness and some kind of mutual understanding. This is a role that depends primarily on the therapist's skills in creating a non-judgemental environment that make it easy for clients to talk and at the same time gives them useful feedback. We all perceive the environment according to the beliefs that we have accepted for ourselves through what we have learned from our environment. We all have our unique ways of categorising both animate and inanimate objects. We see each other through the lens of our own view of the world. My use of the term intrasubjectivity represents this unconscious inner dialogue. Intersubjectivity is different. It is the ability to converse with another person in a way that helps us to understand each other's point of view. We need to find enough common ground in order to work together to achieve a measure of understanding. In psychotherapy therapists are far more equipped to help clients to bring to the surface the source of their troubles when they have already undergone the same process themselves. Then they can remain open enough to avoid the pitfall of trying to persuade clients to a certain point of view instead of helping them to make their own discoveries about what they do or do not need. The first constitutes an unethical use of power and the second, the basis for mutually nurturing cooperation.

NOTES

1. Symptoms are invariably surface manifestations of something that has gone wrong at a deeper level. Once we find the underlying cause and deal with that, the symptoms disappear. This applies to problems in all domains, such as engineering and architecture.

2. There is a long-standing debate about what constitutes unconsciousness and consciousness. Although it is a widespread belief that animals do not have an awareness of consciousness, nevertheless certain non-human mammals are able, for example, to learn what are the best strategies for hunting their prey, through trial and error. This ability implies that they are not ruled by purely instinctive responses. The implication is that thinking does not necessarily depend on the use of language.

3. The desire to study arises out of a strong interest in learning something specific. Without a personal motive to learn it is hard to make progress. To teach children in large groups in a situation where they have to remain seated for long periods and can only proceed at the rate of others in the same group can be very demoralising.

4. Phrases like 'the selfish society' have crept into our common vocabulary. The cry is for people's rights, but we hear little about people's responsibilities. It becomes increasingly apparent that the long-held idealistic belief that once people's basic material needs have been met they will lead happier lives is simply not true. Every day we have evidence that the world is a dangerous place. Many people are not taking enough responsibility for finding a way of living that gives them and their children satisfaction.

   If we are to have a strong sense of personal identity we have to work for it. Like many psychotherapists I find myself getting exasperated by people who talk about low self-esteem, as though it were an illness for which there is a cure. We cannot go and buy a few poundsworth of self-esteem from the supermarket to see ourselves over a difficult period. High self-esteem, as distinct from the ersatz variety, conceit, is something we earn for ourselves through the success of tasks we have set ourselves. There is a true sense of identity which applies itself to the task of how we can best use our inherited physical, mental and emotional resources for our own good both as individuals and as **members** of a community. A false sense of identity is based on the need to please people and conform to community rites and beliefs, not because that is what we want, but to avoid rejection and the consequent angst of being alone in the world.

This is not an argument against what has been called 'the materialistic society'. There is nothing wrong with wanting to save one's time and labour through making use of the advantages of technology. What is wrong is to place too much importance on material objects in the belief that they will make us happy. 'Retail therapy' is another formulaic phrase. If we feel depressed, we can go out and cheer ourselves up by purchasing new clothes. There is nothing wrong with getting pleasure from this activity. However, when it is a substitute for real therapy, which involves facing our problems and recognising that unhappiness is part of everyday life, our behaviour takes on a neurotic, obsessive quality, which cannot lead to true contentment.

We have lost sight of some vital human needs, because we have begun to think of them either as commodities which we can purchase, or as something someone else is refusing to give us, or as something we have a right to without making any effort. These are the kind of remarks heard in everyday conversation that reflect this attitude:

- I could move in with this partner, but what happens if someone better comes along?
- My husband/wife/daughter/boss makes my life difficult
- I do my best for other people but they always treat me badly
- My husband/wife/daughter/boss doesn't understand me
- I've given my husband/wife/son/friends my time and attention but no-on cares about me
- All I want is to be loved
- All I want is to be appreciated
- I don't like the people I am working with
- Everyone lets me down

Every one of these common statements reveals an attitude which could be called 'selfish'. This is a much misunderstood word. Selfishness means avoiding responsibility for our own lives by refusing to recognise our own contributions to relationships, or lack of them, through the dubious tactic of blaming others. Taking care of oneself, means attending to our needs. 'Needs' are vital to our well-being. 'Wants' are not. Wants, more often than not, are temporary boosts to help us to feel better. We need to recognise what we are doing and why.

PART II
The Therapeutic Dialogue in Practice

CHAPTER FIVE

Getting clients to talk

rney & Bergen (1984) brought to our attention that both psychotherapists and doctors were not sufficiently aware of the importance of what they called 'the incitement to talk', with its implications that people who sought help with personal problems needed encouragement to tell their stories. Freud believed that when his patients were incited to talk about whatever comes into their head, the process he called free-association, they will inevitably reveal in the course of time (and it can be a very long time) most aspects of themselves. He considered patients' input as vital in helping them to understand themselves and change what they needed to change. The theory underlying the relative positions of the participants, one lying down on a sofa and the other sitting behind and out of sight; one talking or not-talking[1] and the other listening, is the very antithesis of talk-in-interaction. Yet Freud himself tacitly revealed his awareness of the importance of the therapeutic relationship through his theory of the transference and counter-transference. But then Freud was born into a very different environment, where authoritarianism was rife and 'experts' knew best.

In the 1960s, when Sacks was developing his work, the old class hierarchies were weakening, and the accent was more on people's rights than on their responsibilities. In this climate, the question of power and how it should be used was in the melting pot, making possible a different kind of personal interchange, where people could work together on equal terms even when, at the same time, one person acknowledges the need for professional knowledge and guidance. Respect for other people is an underlying principle in all Sacks' lecture notes.

The professional dominance[2] idea belongs to the past, yet so strong was its influence that it lingers on in some aspects of professional training. Freud's prescription was that therapists should not speak first. They should listen, echo back clients' words to them, and make no comments of their own apart from interpretations. Moreover, the belief that therapists should not talk about their own experiences, lest their attention should stray away from their clients to themselves, lingers on in some areas of training.

The roots of our individual character are embedded in our genetic inheritance and its interaction with our experiences of the world including other people, a topic I explored in Chapter Four. Self-awareness can be acquired only through on-going monitoring of ourselves in all our behaviour with other people. However, much of this information is available only to our unconscious minds. A life-shaking shock may sometimes jolt us into the conscious knowledge of previously unrecognised facets of ourselves. However, our defence mechanisms are powerful and well entrenched, since their purpose is to hide from us aspects of ourselves that threaten a carefully constructed, unrealistic view of ourselves. It takes a trained professional, well versed in tried-and-proven psychological theory, with exceptionally developed interrelational skills, gifted with the powers of insight, the ability to make connections and find patterns, to help clients to understand themselves better. All human behaviour is understandable when we have identified the underlying motivation for our actions.

So how do we, as therapists, know when we have found the source of the problem? When we have arrived at a consensus with our clients and when clients, acting on this knowledge, begin to make the changes that help to free them from long-standing neuroses. None of this can be achieved unless therapists are able to collect relevant clues to the problem from what clients tell them. People will not talk freely unless they feel they are accepted and respected by non-judgemental therapists. First, an ambience of rapport must be established. If it is not achieved, despite all efforts, then clients may need a change of therapist. In this business there are horses for courses.

These are the reasons why getting clients to talk is the first and most important aspect of psychotherapy. In **interviews**, questions usually play a large part, since they are the most obvious ways of getting information. However, direct questioning, especially strings of questions, can feel threatening to recipients. As we have emphasised, people who come for therapy have painful problems that they have been unable to work out for themselves. Dealing with sensitive material requires a sensitive approach. Therefore it did not surprise me when conducting my research that far fewer questions are asked in my data than might have been expected.

Questions are not only syntactic devices to get information. They can also be used for other purposes, to issue invitations for example:

(1)
```
B: Why don't you come and see me some [times
A:                                     [I would like to.
B: I would like you to. Lemme [just
A:                            [I don't know just where
   the-uh-this address is.
   (Schegloff, 1984, p. 31)
```

Questions can be useful in many different ways. In this book I restrict myself to those that are relevant to the task of therapy.

First I shall describe different ways in which therapists can encourage clients to talk. Second, I shall suggest how some of these devices could be applied to everyday conversation to help all those people who have difficulty in meeting new people and starting conversations.

Getting clients to talk by asking questions

Questions can be divided into two types, open and closed.[3] Both are used in psychotherapy. In psychotherapy training students are encouraged to ask **open questions** in the belief that they place fewer constraints on answers. They offer more freedom of response than

closed questions. The emphasis is on the 'incitement to speak'. There are varying degrees of openness and closedness. They are at opposite ends of a spectrum. At one end is a question which invites only one answer, 'yes' or 'no' as in the following:

(2) [JP/Edb]
```
T: And was he self-employed? =
C: =Yes.
```

At the other end is a question with a lesser constraint: clients can say what they like provided they stay within the boundary of "since you came last time":

(3) [JP/Ma4/5898]
```
Q  T:  ...Okay. So (.) how (.) since you came last time
       (.) how have things been?
A  C:  .hhh we:ll (4.6) .hhh (.) well (0.8) it's an
       Interesting mixed bag...
       ((laughing tone))
       (C begins an extended turn)
```

This type of **open question** usually produces a response, since clients can easily remember recent events and are eager to talk about them, especially if they can tell their therapists that they are making changes as in the following example:

(4) [JP/M3/8201]
```
 1  T:  Minna. How have you been since last time you ca[me?
 2  C:                                                 [Okay
 3      yes - seems like a long time ago actu[ally
 4  T:                                        [It does seem
 5      a long time doesn't it?=
 6  C:  = Yes.
 7  T:  What is it - two =
 8  C:  = Yes it's only two weeks =
 9  T:  = Yes =
10  C:  = in fact I've done a lot of reading and I've done
11      a lot of (1.7) I dunno really everything just seems
12      (.) to have been (.) easier.
13  T:  (.) Does it? =
14  C:  = but the stupid thing is it seems easier =
15  T:  = Yes =
16  C:  = cos I just-because I had a different attitude ...
       (followed by a detailed description in examples (2) and (3)
       in Chapter Six)
```

Asking for information about any changes clients have noticed between sessions is a particularly useful device in psychotherapy. It cannot, of course, be used to open up a first session, but in all subsequent sessions it has two helpful purposes. Clients have a chance to comment on their afterthoughts about the previous session, and they can tell stories that illustrate ongoing change. Since clients choose the topics of their talk, they exercise their right to say what they want to say and therefore speak freely.

Both example (3) and (4) show that an **open question** can lead to a client beginning to tell a story. However this does not always happen. Here is an example where it takes three questions to get the client to talk:

(5) [JP/Ma5/4598]
```
    C: I've been sort of - a bit confused as to what
       I want to be sort of doing.
Q1  T: How has this affected your life? I mean in
       your ordinary everyday experience with
       people. What have you been doing?
       (1.5)
A1  C: hh um
       (8.0)
Q2  T: T: Have you been confused in your interactions
       with people?=
A2  C: =a bit - yes=
Q3  T: =Right then. And er never knowing how to
       behave or what to say?=
A3  C: Yeah. Because I know that - on the one hand
       There's a way I want to be behaving but on
       the other hand there's - like something else
       (.) sort of how to behave another way. In
       fact I went to the (    ) supermarket
       yesterday..........
       (story follows)
```

Here Q1 is an open question, followed by a pause of (1.5) seconds, then by ".hh um" which is not so much a response as an indication that a response might be forthcoming. However, instead of C embarking on a topic initiation, there is a very long pause of (8.0) seconds. T waits patiently for a reply, displaying that she recognises C has something to say but seems to have difficulty in so doing.[4]

Q2 is a more specific question and receives a prompt, qualified affirmative, "a bit - yes" (A2). But it is only when a third, Q3, more

closed question narrows the options down to two, "never knowing how to behave or what to say", that C takes up one of the two options, "not knowing how to behave" as the topic of the story he begins to tell. This is a clear example where an open question is not successful, but when the questions become more specific, the client begins to talk.

Questions 2 and 3 are examples of what Jefferson (1988) and Wowk (1989) describe as **candidate elaborations** when therapists assist clients to describe their problems more clearly by suggesting possible meanings of clients' generalisations. Candidate elaborations are very useful in helping clients to talk. They will be discussed more fully in Chapter Seven.

The use of therapists' self-disclosure in getting clients to talk

The idea that therapists should not reveal details about their own lives is another traditional principle that is fading too slowly. It offers clients the hope that they too can recover from setbacks and improve the quality of their lives. Sacks (1992) argues that it is not possible to listen attentively without being constantly reminded of one's own experiences.

Sacks (1992) claims that listening to be reminded is a naturally occurring phenomenon, evidenced by the analysis of first and second stories. One speaker telling a story reminds the recipient of something that happened to her/him. A second story is then produced whose structure is similar to the first. Patients like to talk with someone who has had the same experiences as themselves. It reassures them that they are not going mad. **Self-disclosure** is another example of what Jefferson (1986) calls pre-affiliation, where the recipients encourage first speakers to give further detail by exhibiting that they have had the same experiences.

An interactive style in therapy is now recognised as valuable for helping clients to remember what they need to say. McLeod (2000) describes the emergence of **narrative therapy** as a therapeutic method for helping people to make sense of their experience.

In my data there are examples of therapists talking about their own experience. I shall now give some examples to show some different types of disclosures and the use clients make of them. In some cases **self-disclosure** and information are combined.

The following two examples illustrate self-disclosure. In all cases the clients' responses constitute the opening of an extended sequence of self-analysis. In example (6) this occurs at the onset of a consultation. T is having difficulty operating her audio recorder. This is the first time she has used it to record a therapy session:

(6) [JP/Ma/4598]

```
 1 T: Oh yes. It's going. Yes. I don't understand
 2     the ways of these machines - Okay (.) So (.)
 3     I'm a complete idiot in some ways. It's
 4     very good to be a complete idiot - you don't
 5     feel so superior to others - it's very easy
 6     to feel superior to others when you have a
 7     little bit more knowledge than they have.
 8     Okay. About making a fool of oneself. Is that
 9     something you can do easily?
10 C: Making a fool of myself depends on context -
11     and if I'm in a situation where I don't mind
12     making a fool of myself that's fine - I mean
13     - it's er - I mean -it's sort of like a
14     pretend status loss but it isn't really a
15     status loss because it entirely depends on
16     what sort of circumstances and the people you
17     are with...
```

Hutchby & Moran-Ellis (2001) pose the question "what role might the technological device itself play in the unfolding of the session?" (Hutchby & Moran Ellis, 2001, p. 116) Hutchby found that some counsellors he met during his research thought that the presence of audio recorders might inhibit the production of 'natural' talk. This presupposes that there is such a thing as a 'normative model of counselling'. The turn-taking structure of the talk-in-interaction in psychotherapy depends on the problem under investigation. The speech-exchange system is created moment by moment through the interaction of the participants. Hutchby examines the effect that the presence of the tape-recorder may or may not have on the character of the talk-in-interaction.

The effect on the opening lines of example (6) of the presence of the tape-recorder, and T's difficulty in getting it going, is that T refers to this problem out loud. The acknowledgement of her own ineptness is incorporated into the preface to her first question (lines 8–9).

T switches her **footing**[5] three times in her extended turn (lines 1–9). She first talks out loud to herself as she attempts to get the machine working (lines 1–3). She then addresses herself to C and transforms the notion of being 'a complete idiot' to a skill (lines 3–7). Finally she asks C a question based on her reframing. It is hard to imagine this kind of device with its reversal of 'what everyone knows', (i.e., the belief that to play the fool is a bad thing) being immediately accepted in mundane conversation. Yet C responds at once and in detail, taking up the topic of "making a fool of oneself", and producing an elaboration that includes some informative comments about how he sees things. T's transformation of "making a fool of oneself" to a skill succeeds in providing an area of comfort in which C can discuss a sensitive issue. The proof of this is that not only does C respond promptly, but he also begins a lengthy discussion on the topic.

The next fragment takes place some twenty minutes into the consultation. T has just finished imparting information to C and marks the conclusion with a request for feedback on her own style:

(7) [JP/Ma2/11598] Extract from Appendix 2:3
```
 1  T:  Okay.Right.°I've been talking a lot again°.hh
 2      um (.) Do you think I talk too
 3      much? >cos when I've looked into some of my
 4      tapes I think there's an awful lot of me on it<
 5      Is it help[ful?
 6  C:            [.hhh Oh I think it is cos it
 7      stimulates ideas in me too =
 8  T:  = _Good. [That's] what I'm hoping. Yes. [Yes
 9  C:          [ Mmm ]                         [and I
10      think that's good as well and it helps me to
11      understand things an[d I] think it probably =
12  T:                      [Yes]
13  C:  = reinforces things that I already think
14      anyway[( )] things that I do thin[k but] it =
15  T:        [Mmm]                        [uhum ]
16  C:  = just sort of y'know brings them to the
17      the forefront of my mind and then I think that
18      probably helps just sort of going over it
19       simp - y'know just sort of what you said about
20      (.) doing things that I find interesting.
21  T:  Yes.
22  C:  Yeah. And I mean I think that's DEAD RIGHT.
```

Again, in this example, the use of the tape recorder has an effect on the opening lines. This time T refers to what she has learned about her own style through listening to the first tape she has recorded from the previous session with C. As in example (6), this piece of **self-disclosure**, serves as a preface to her first question (lines 2–3).

As in example (6), T moves from one footing to another in her first turn. She talks softly to herself (line 1). This is followed by the intake of breath (.hh) and 'um'. This serves as a **buffer device** (Hutchby, 1999) indicating that she is about to embark on a topic. T then asks a question (first change of footing, line 2), then self-discloses (second change of footing, lines 3 and 4), then asks another question (third change of footing).

It is an oft repeated rule in therapy training that therapists do not worry clients with their own problems, yet this is what T is doing. However, seen in the light that the only way T can find out if her 'talking too much' as she sees it, is contraindicative for the work, is to ask C. Then her self-disclosure and request for feedback can be seen as relevant for the task.

C's eagerness to reply (line 7) makes visible his willingness to give feedback to T. What is more he has plenty to say, going into considerable detail and closing with a robust confirmation of his own evaluation in the final line 22. His response demonstrates that T's self-disclosure has been useful for him in several ways, reinforcing what he already thinks and bringing his thoughts "to the forefront of my mind" (line 17). This particular extract demonstrates the strong sense of solidarity that can be engendered in clients when therapists reveal things about themselves that could be seen as weaknesses. They pick up the tacit understanding that if therapists can accept themselves, then they can accept their clients and avoid making judgements.

Thus self-disclosure can be a source of various therapeutic devices. It can demonstrate to the client that he is not alone with his problem, it can give him the confidence to discuss sensitive issues more easily and it can reinforce the **affiliation** between the participants. This theme will be explored further in Chapter Seven.

How to encourage people to talk in everyday conversation

A common reason for seeking therapy is a lack of social skills in interpersonal relationships. A new client called me up and said he was suffering from 'social phobia', a term I had not come across before. When we met I asked him where he had learned it. "From the Internet" he replied. I laughed and said "Not another bit of psycho-babble.

We've got far too much of that already. Tell me what you mean by it." He then explained that he had always been shy. I asked him to explain what that particular lexical item meant to him. He said he did not know what to say when talking to strangers. This was not true. The underlying reason was that he was so worried about what other people would think about him that he was afraid to say anything at all in case he caused offence to another.

Many people suffer from this problem. My own way of working with it is two faceted. I help clients to identify the source of their fear and at the same time give them simple exercises to do that will help them to develop conversation skills. The first is the most important. Whenever we have a strong emotional reaction to a situation, logical thought flies out of the window. Emotions and instincts give the impression of 'rightness', because they have been with us forever, from the earliest time that the forbears of human beings came into existence. Once our ancestors developed the ability to speak they began to think in a more sophisticated way.[6]

However, because our emotional responses to events depend on what we have learned, they have a ring of truth about them that is unrealistic. Our beliefs cause trouble when they are not something we have worked out for ourselves but are the result of how we have been affected by other people in the earliest stages of our existence, our childhood. Sacks gives a very explicit explanation of how we develop beliefs, through the injunctions imposed on children by adults, that lay down unhelpful patterns for our thinking and cause us trouble in later life. This finding, based on his own observations of human behaviour, enabled him to appreciate the soundness of Freud's principle of psychodynamics, the method of relating patterns of behaviour and thinking to early social conditioning.

My client, having avoided doing things he feared, a very natural human reaction, had had very little practice in knowing how to open up talk with a stranger, and what to talk about after the ice was broken. The situation was worsened by his reluctance to go to places where he knew he would have the chance to meet others.

This is a common problem that is based on a matrix of beliefs that undermine our sense of identity and reinforce a fear of rejection. We have gradually absorbed these beliefs at an unconscious level. Therefore in order to tackle them we first need bring them up to the surface. Neither of these feelings are illnesses, so no one else can 'cure' them. The difficulty with labels like 'social phobia', is that they convince people something is 'wrong' with them and someone else can put it 'right'. My belief is that in psychotherapy we do not do 'cures'. We help people to identify their faulty beliefs and consequent behaviours by analysing how they developed in the first place. Once that is done, it then becomes possible for clients to make changes in the way they think about their lives.

How we identify clients' beliefs is by listening carefully to what they say. We make use of language when we tell stories about our lives that reveal the habits of thought and behaviour we have acquired through our responses to life experiences from birth onwards. How therapists do this is the subject of Chapter Six.

We use up a lot of energy in order to keep ourselves in a state of continual worry. This involves what a client of mine called 'self-dwell'. Wrapped up in our own unhappiness we hear every word of the internal, negative dialogue we are producing and fail to notice how others are responding to us. Therefore we have no resources left for paying attention to other people.

Helping clients to bring unrecognised beliefs to the surface is an important part of psychotherapy. All people who have this problem of 'shyness' could benefit from therapy provided that they find a therapist they can work with. Certain therapists' skills that help them to get clients to talk can be applied to how we can start a conversation with people we have not met before. Before I move on to this topic, I shall say something about why talking with other people seems to be the source of so many difficulties.

What we all need from other people

Without other people we would never discover our identity. We cannot love, hate, help, teach, reject or accept in a vacuum. It is through our interactions with other people that we discover ourselves. In our complex society we are dependent on a vast army of other people, most of whom we never meet. Without food, water, heating, transport, all things we take for granted, we should not survive. We have come a long way from our earlier animal existence, when we only needed to belong to a small society, where every animal knew every other animal in their group, and all cooperated for the common good.

Even as recently as the period preceding the industrial revolution, people lived in small communities. Each adult was proficient in one type of work. Butcher, baker, candlestick-maker, blacksmith, cartwright, and farmer all contributed their special skills, which were often passed down from father to son. True, they were subservient to overall government, but each village was an independent entity that worked well.

The rules of exponential growth ensure that the more we develop new technologies, the faster we move towards more sophisticated levels of innovation. Individuals become more and more dependent on new services that make our lives easier. Fewer and fewer people are getting the satisfaction of doing one job from start to finish. What we gain from an easier life seems to make our individual lives more complex and less satisfying. Hence the exponential growth of what we now call 'mental-illness'[7] and the increasing number of psychotherapists and counsellors.

In earlier times, it was sufficient for us to learn to get on with a small number of people in a slowly developing environment. We have to adapt to an ever-increasing number of changes: meeting many more people, learning to relate to a new society and making new friends if the requirements of our work mean that we have to move to a different place several times in our lives, with all the consequent upheaval and readjustment.

All people need to be valued for themselves, to be accepted for who they are, to find a social group of friends with whom they have enough in common to be able have enjoyable conversations that reflect their level of knowledge and intelligence and gives them the opportunity to make a significant contribution to that group. In order to do this we need to be able to make assessments about people we meet so that we can decide what kind of relationship, if any, we should like to have with them.

We cannot do this without a realistic idea of our own value. Many clients' difficulties are expressed in such formulaic statements as 'low self-esteem', 'no self-confidence', 'if people really got to know me they wouldn't like me.' A common expectation is that with my knowledge of hypnosis I can put everything right without them having to do anything themselves. Before I take on clients I make it quite clear that they are the only ones who can make changes by using my expertise to help them to help themselves. There are only two things I ask: that they should have the courage to explore their own painful issues, under my guidance, and be prepared to take action. There are many ways in which we can all learn to behave differently in our interactions with other people.

How do we behave and talk to other people in order to find out something about them?

Going back to Chapter Four, remember the most important factor is the therapeutic relationship, which itself is based on rapport. Rapport is established when both parties feel at ease with each other and can speak freely. This is true in ordinary conversation as well as in psychotherapy.

The primary requirement for being able to talk to another person spontaneously is to be genuinely interested in them. Therefore, when you open up a conversation with someone you do not know, it is essential that you give them your full attention. In order to do this you need to forget about yourself and focus on the other person. The three key things to remember are notice, notice, notice. Keep eye contact and watch carefully so that you are aware of body language including details such as where the client's gaze is directed. Listen carefully not only to hear but to notice how it is said. Tone of voice (warm or neutral), hesitations, self-corrections, and what kind of responses are given to what you are saying will all give you valuable information.

Stay focused on the person to whom you are talking. Never ask yourself what that person is thinking about you. You cannot know, and in any case it is irrelevant. Regard this as an exercise in information gathering that will add to your skills in understanding other people and yourself better. Remember that for everyone our favourite subject is ourselves, and anyone who listens intently to us talking about ourselves will gain our goodwill.

If you operate on the assumption that no-one will like you, you will convey this message through the way you behave and it will turn out to be true, a self-fulfilling prophecy. If that person reminds you of someone you dislike, tell yourself that this is a new person and you know nothing about them. Notice that open questions sometimes are unhelpful in getting clients to talk. Often the introduction of a few **closed questions** will help clients to find a topic they can discuss. Both of these apply to everyday conversation. The asking of questions needs to be undertaken with care. It is not difficult to convince people you are interrogating them and no-one likes that.

Avoid old clichés like 'do you come here often?' Instead start with a story that has some relevance to the situation and gives the addressee a chance to be reminded of another. Avoid telling long rambling stories that have no relevance. Whatever you say must be designed specifically for the person you are addressing. If it is not, you will give the message that you are only interested in yourself.

You can very easily acquire a reputation for friendliness and charm when you talk to someone with that level of concentration that gives them the impression that they are the only one in the room. As soon as you set out to please, which usually means you are trying to make a good impression by giving them what you think they want when you haven't the faintest idea of what that is, you are doomed to failure. Forgetfulness of self and spontaneity is all.

Conclusion

In this chapter I have given examples of different ways in which therapists can help clients to feel comfortable enough to talk freely about what is troubling them. Because psychotherapy is a professional service sought out by people who need help in understanding their lives, there is a considerable constraint on therapists to pay considerable attention to gain their trust. Many people have trouble in opening conversation with someone they have not met before. I am arguing the case that if we make the same effort to get others to talk to us in ordinary conversation, focusing not on ourselves, but on the person we are addressing, we can easily overcome this particular problem.

In Chapter Six we shall go on to the next stage in therapy when the way the participants talk together changes as clients begin to open up and tell their stories.

NOTES

1. Quite a lot of 'not talking' can take place in psychoanalysis. A client may lie curled up on the sofa in a blanket and say nothing for the entire session. This is considered to serve a useful purpose. What that is I have no idea. Despite my having made numerous enquiries into this matter, no-one has presented me with a convincing argument for its usefulness.

2. Heath (1992) reminds us that the doctor/patient relationship has been traditionally seen as an asymmetric relationship dominated by the doctor. The belief was that only the professional could make a diagnosis and prescribe treatment because he alone has access to knowledge of how the body works and everyone's body operates on the same principles. Ten Have (1991) argues that **professional dominance** lingers on in medicine. He shows how patients themselves contribute to the asymmetric position through attitudes they have assimilated from tradition. This is radically different from the practice of psychotherapy, where the workings of the mind vary with individuals, and diagnosis is jointly agreed. Nevertheless, because the medical model for diagnosis and treatment preceded the practice of psychotherapy, it has had a knock-on effect on psychotherapy. Because of the differences between each and every one human being, I believe psychotherapy cannot be seen as a science. It is an art.

3. The only research I have found that examines the work done by open and closed questions is, not surprisingly, in the site of the classroom. Wood (1995) summarises the major findings. There are interesting similarities and differences between the two sites of teaching and therapy which help to highlight some facets that are peculiar to psychotherapy. Both institutions use more closed than open questions. In education they serve to teach facts. In therapy they seek information about facts and in addition information about the feelings and emotions of clients. In both cases the identification of factual information brought about by closed questions serves useful purposes.

   Open questions in teaching help children to "speculate, hypothesize and discuss more." As we have noted, in therapy open questions can be problematic and sometimes need to be followed by a series of closed questions in order to facilitate the flow of talk. The differences in the two situations, that in teaching one is talking to many and in therapy to only one, means that in therapy any discussion can only be between two people.

In the one-to-one situation "the synchronization is finely tuned". Having only one person to focus on enables therapists to pick up clues by means of, for example, allowing waiting time for the clients' answers. This is much harder to do in the classroom. Wood's conclusion is that "discourse controlled by teacher questions that often demand quick terse, factual answers ... leaves little time for children to respond, elaborate or reason out loud". Children do not learn how to "say what they know". In contrast, the opposite is true in therapy. Clients are encouraged to "say what they know" so clues can be picked up more easily. Therapists have more freedom to organise how they position questions and what kind of questions they ask at any particular point.

4. The reasons for long pauses between utterances can be difficult to ascertain. Sometimes it is useful to wait for a reply. At other times it may be wiser for the therapist to jump in and intervene. It all depends on the therapist's individual skills and their knowledge of a particular client.

5. Goffman (1979) uses the term 'footing' to describe the particular action that a speaker is doing at any point during a conversation. Examples of such actions include questioning, listening, talking to oneself, making suggestions and encouraging someone to talk.

6. There is an ongoing debate about the actual process of thinking. Some believe that animals cannot think because they cannot talk. Yet there are arguments that suggest we do not need words to think. Animals manage to work out strategies for survival. Wittgenstein (1953) discusses the difficulties that ensue when we try to find a definition for the process of thinking. In psychotherapy such approaches as cognitive therapy and neuro-linguistic programming and Sacks' work in the social sciences point to the profound effect of language on the way we interpret our feelings. We have managed to build up a wide range of different labels for our emotions, which we could not have done before language existed. The attribution of meaning to these definitions distorts the perception of our instinctive reactions and complicates both how we understand our emotional reactions and the way we conduct our lives.

7. Szaz's (1962) seminal work, *The Myth of Mental Illness* challenged the concept that certain kinds of behaviour could be treated as though they were physical disorders of the body. Like Korzybski (1933) he believed that the complexity of our adaptation to modern society, especially the way we use language, is a major cause of what is called 'mental illness.' Simeon's (1960) book *Man's Presumptuous Brain* is an evolutionary interpretation of psychosomatic

disease, that explains this highly prevalent condition as the conflict between our instinctive reactions to stress and the pressures that arise from our difficulties in adapting our lives to rapidly advancing change through the ever-increasing complexity of technology. The fact remains that it is still extremely difficult to differentiate between genuine bodily illness and psychosomatic symptoms.

CHAPTER SIX

Troubles-telling

Story-telling is a feature of everyday conversation that has been analysed for its structural, sequential and interactional properties by Jefferson (1978, 1988) and Goodwin (1984). It is a special kind of speech-exchange system where one person acts as story-teller and one or more participants act as recipients. Stories can be carriers for accounts of troubles. As Sacks (1992) has noted, " 'troubles-talk' is the base focus of Western literature" (Sacks, 1992, p. 230–231) since it is much richer and more varied than "the poverty of normality". Such accounts are conversationally generative, providing topics that can be talked about at length. Therefore troubles-talk can be a valuable source for the gathering of information about clients' problems.

In this chapter, I shall develop four themes: the responses of the listener, the troubles-telling itself, the unpacking of the meaning of the troubles-telling, and the differences between troubles-telling in psychotherapy and story-telling in everyday conversation.

The therapist's responses to the troubles-telling

The unfolding of a troubles-telling requires responses from the hearer, who in the following case is the therapist. A passive acceptance offers nothing to the speaker. Rapport will not be established if the client feels that the therapist is not interested enough to give appropriate feedback. Sacks gives an example of passive reception. The setting is an emergency psychiatric clinic, which takes telephone calls from people who feel suicidal. The participants are a doctor and a caller/patient.

"(1)
```
pt. I've got a date coming in a half hour and I (sob)
dr. I see
pt. I can't go through with it. I can't go through the
    evening I can't (sniffle)
dr. uh huh
pt. You talk I don't want to talk
dr. Uh huh
pt. (laugh sob) It sounds like a real professional uh
    huh uh huh (sniffle)" (Sacks, 1992, p. 387–388)
```

In this extract, the patient displays annoyance at the responses of the doctor. "It sounds like a real professional" is clearly not meant as a compliment. This kind of response in ordinary conversation would be taken as unfeeling, showing no sympathy. As a result of the poverty of the responses the caller decides that she does not want to talk. Bearing in mind that getting clients to talk is a necessity if anything is going to be achieved in the way of therapy, the doctor's responses are anything but helpful.

You do not have to be a psychologist to realise that the patient sees the repeated "uh huh" as a stereotypical way of responding that does not take account of what she is saying. Sacks argues that the listener's close attention to the design of responses by reference to what is being told is necessary for the maintenance of **affiliation**. A diversity of responses is an active way of showing clients they are being heard. The point is that listening attentively involves the design of responses that reveal, at the very least, an effort to understand what has been said, and awareness of clients' wishes.

This is an important example of how Sacks challenged some of the assumptions about psychotherapy in the 1960s. Whenever anyone is telling a story, the nature of the listener's responses encourages the story-teller by demonstrating that they are heard with effortfulness. Thus even a story-telling which involves one person doing most of the talking, is jointly produced. The nature of the responses has an effect on the way the story is told.

Continuers

The purpose of **continuers, appositionals** such as 'yes', 'Mm' and 'uh huh' is to encourage clients to keep talking. However, as we can see in example (1), they can have the opposite effect when inappropriately placed. The sequential nature of all conversations requires that responses should constitute an acknowledgement of what has just been said, in a way that contributes to ongoing mutual understanding. In this example "uh huh" in response to "You talk I don't want to talk" fails to succeed in eliciting information from the patient and results in the patient making a critical comment about the uselessness of the doctor's responses that brings the talk to a full stop.

Jefferson & Lee (1992) helped me to be aware of the difference between **alignment** and affiliation. **Alignment** is displayed by the way the respondent recognises what topic is being discussed. By its very nature it is neutral. It shows that the recipient understands what the speaker is trying to say, and gives the speaker the chance to correct if the recipient has 'got it wrong'.

Affiliation, in strong contrast to alignment, is emotional. When troubles-telling occurs in everyday conversation, the expectation of the teller is that a sympathetic response will be evoked. When it occurs in what the authors call 'a service encounter', that is in a situation where one person is seeking professional help from another, the expectations are different. Service seekers, potential clients and patients, are looking for guidance to help them to understand what has gone wrong and how they can put it right. Therefore alignment to the topic under discussion is very important.

The point made by the authors is that responses can be unhelpful unless they are appropriately chosen for a specific purpose. Whilst **affiliative responses** are acceptable in ordinary conversation, they can be disruptive in therapy talk. Clients do not need sympathy, they need help in solving their problems. They are paying for a service and they want to feel they are getting value for their money.

Yet the failure to give an **affiliative response**, as in example (1), can also disrupt the smooth progress of sequential talk. The authors opine that what matters is that whether the response shows alignment or affiliation, it should be appropriate to that particular place where it is used. This is itself an art that recognises both the need for a neutral exploration of a problem and "the deeply remedial potential of emotional reciprocity" (Jefferson & Lee, 1992, p. 546).

Responses that incorporate both alignment and affiliation

Affiliative responses are particularly helpful in situations where clients are displaying progress in making changes and coming to new realisations about themselves. There is a caveat here. The constraining factor in everything therapists say should be the relevance to the task of therapy. However, in the initial phases of therapy, it is often difficult to know what is relevant and what is not. Different topics can be explored and lead nowhere. That is inevitable in the early stages. Clients may try to get agreement from therapists when therapists, basing their judgement on what clients have already said, feel that they cannot agree. To do this would be collusion and unhelpful to clients.[1]

So how do therapists know when to agree and when not to agree? This question highlights the importance of listening for clues. Agreements are **warranted** when therapists are careful to make their own judgements on the basis of what has already happened in the therapy sessions. For this reason the following examples have all been chosen at a later point in the therapeutic work when both therapist and client are getting closer to understanding the problem. Once that has happened, maintaining and generating alignment and affiliation becomes easier for the therapist. When alignment and affiliation become fused, as in the following examples, they display a felicitous combination of a neutral, cognitive recognition of the meaning of the client's prior turn and a warm feeling response that gives emotional validity to what has been said.

The particle 'yes' can both serve to encourage clients to go on talking and to confirm the changes they are making, as in the following example:

```
(2) [JP/M3/8201]
1     C:  ...because I thought well I'll look at this book=
2  →  T:  =Yes=
3     C:  =and I've got to READ the Boo[k ] I must=
4  →  T:                               [Yes]
5     C:  =read this book >these are the books you HAVE
6         to read them<=
7  →  T:  =Yes=
8     C:  =but I haven't DONE that. I've read a piece of the
```

```
9         book and [that's] started me off on something else=
10 →  T:             [ Yes ]
11 →  T: =Yes.
```

C demonstrates how she is changing the way she studies. Her previous attitude, that she felt obliged to read the set books (lines 5–6)
contrasts with her new strategy in lines 8–9. C's utterance flows
freely as one statement. She does not need five 'yes' **continuers** to
help her to keep going. One alone would do when she has finished
speaking but the four extra 'yes' particles serve to reinforce T's recognition that she is doing well.

Later in the same transcript:

(3)
```
1     C: And the people y'know like (.) um (.) was - this
2        y'know (.) °Gestalt?°
3  →  T: Oh yes (.) yes (.) Gestalt=
4     C: =Yes Gestalt (.) and I've been reading a lot of
5        stuff and- and - and the people I've been reading
6        like Ronald Lai [ng (.)he] was talking about=
7  →  T:                 [Oh yes ]
8     C: =counselling as an art form instead of - er-
9        scientific=
10 →  T: =Yes=
11    C: =and a LOT of people that I've READ were
12       mentioned in this book about Gestalt theory.
13 →  T: Right
14    C: I raked out all the old books. (.) looked at
15       what they said about it [ (    )
16 →  T:                         [Yes and you're getting
17       it and you're beginning to enjoy it for its own
         sake.
```

Encouraged by T's affiliative reception of her progress, C begins to
expand on the changes she has made in the way she works in greater
detail. T continues to respond warmly and finishes with a **candidate
elaboration** (see Chapter Seven) showing that she understands the
pleasure C is getting from her new way of studying.

Sometimes encouragement can be upgraded as in the following
examples:

(4a) [JP/E2/28299]
```
1     C: I don't want to grow up! The clingy one again
         y'know=
2  →  T: =Exactly. Yes. Exactly. Yes.
```

(b) [JP/M2]

```
1    C: And a lot of people say "Well that's it. It's
2       finished. I'll leave it to my doctors.
3       Whatever happens, happens." =
4  → T: =ExACTly. Well you're not taking that - attitude.
5    C: NO::
```

'Exactly' is a stronger response than 'yes'. When used sparingly, its effect is greater, confirming and enhancing C's conclusions, and reinforcing the difference between the routine 'yes' and the more categorical 'exactly'. The following example shows an even stronger response:

(5) [JP/Ma]

```
1    C: ...Because earlier on I've been shifting
2       responsibility to everybody else because
3       it's a perceived criticism on their part=
4  → T: =Ex[actly        [Yes]
5    C:    [But really [I'm] doing it.
6  → T: Yes. Great insight. Absolutely great! Good.
```

Readers may perhaps feel that line 6 is a bit over-the-top. However, the enthusiasm of T's response, with four different receipts, represents an exceptional response to an exceptionally acute insight. One of those moments that make therapists want to jump for joy is when clients, after a long period of work in therapy sessions, finally recognise that they alone are responsible for themselves, and stop blaming external objects, be they people or events, for their problems. The recognition that it is not what happens to us but how we handle it that matters is all important.

In example (1) it could be said that there is only one way that this particular doctor is aligned: by being willing to take the telephone call, and give a series of neutral responses that do not succeed in getting the caller to talk. Sacks' recognition that conversation is a jointly produced, made-on-the-spot activity, where meaning is created through the ways the participants respond to each other must, by definition preclude the repetition of a series of stereotypical responses.

The very nature of psychotherapy, where clients' problems are shrouded in faulty thinking linked with confused emotions and/ or psychosomatic symptoms, requires two kinds of responses from therapists: those that demonstrate alignment with the topic under discussion, and those that demonstrate affiliation by supporting and encouraging clients' discoveries about themselves and the consequent changes they make in their lives.

Change-of-state tokens

Therapists use a device called **change-of-state tokens,** to display their recognition that clients have given them new information. Atkinson & Heritage (1984) have shown that the particle 'oh' is a response that exhibits a 'change of state' in the mind of the recipient. It can constitute a display of surprise on the receipt of news. There are phrases that comprise two different **receipt tokens** such as 'oh I see' and 'oh right' and have greater impact. 'Really' is a stronger token because, like the particle 'oh' it displays surprise. The following fragments illustrate this point. They move from simple acknowledgements of news to stronger **receipt tokens:**

(6a) [JP/Ma/2a]
```
1     C: I think it's different [ (.)  I] think=
2  →  T:                        [Oh right]
3     C: =it's more to do with...
```

(b) [JP/M/11101]
```
1     C: I just had it in my mind that it was
2        going to be (.) the IDEAL Chrismas=
3  →  T: = Oh I see=
4     C: = and all the family's going to be there.
```

(c) [P/Ed/B]
```
1     C: I (.) realised that I hadn't (.) experimented
2        with a lot of feelings.
3  →  T: REALLY?
```

(d) [JP/M2]
```
1     C: ...but once we'd worked through that (.) and
2        got that OVER with (.) during the next couple
3        of weeks=
4     T: =Yes=
5     C: =I thought of all the nice things that
6        ha[ppened
7  →  T:   [REALLY? Did you?
```

These variants in strength of response serve as **markers** that display different degrees of importance given to the news by the therapist, and constitute useful feedback for the client because they emphasise certain events, which bring them to clients' attention.

Paralinguistic responses

Paralinguistic responses are not lexical items, they are sounds such as weeping or laughing that are in themselves responses. I shall confine myself to the most pervasive feature of this type of response in my data, laughter, a topic that has been extensively explored by Jefferson (1979, 1984). Jefferson (1984) notes that "recipient laughter by reference to prior speaker's laughter is a recurrent phenomenon in ordinary conversation". (Jefferson, 1984 p. 348) The following example occurs in troubles-telling and illustrates that phenomenon noted by Jefferson (1984): teller displaying he/she is in good spirits by treating the trouble lightly and inviting the recipient to join in the laughter:

```
(7) [JP/E/28299]
 1    T: Yes (.) just as you say (.) experimenting
 2       (.)learning how to get on with the opposite sex.
 3    C: Also I still (.) also have problems with men
 4       as well but it doesn (.) it doesn't worry me
 5 →    h[uh huh
 6    T: [.h huh hahahahaha. What kind of problems did
 7       you have with men?=
 8    C: =not only does it not worry me but I think
 9       I have a lot more experience with men because
10       I can't help but bump into them. ((laughing tone))
11    T: .h huh hahahaha (.) but it's not so easy to
12       bump into women .hh hahahaha.
13    C: God no! It's not so easy to...
         (C begins a troubles-telling) (Jefferson, 1984, p. 351)
```

In this example C initiates the invitation to laugh. T joins in as a preface to taking up C's comment on his problems with men. C continues in joking fashion in lines 8–10. This ends on a serious note in line 13, when C begins to talk at length about his difficulties in adolescence. The reciprocal jokes and laughter of both therapist and client lighten the atmosphere of the therapy session and make it easier for C to proceed with his troubles-telling.

Later on in the same tape T initiates the humour:

(8) [JP/E/28299]
```
 1    C: ...I just haven't had (.) much experience
 2       with (1.8) um (.) relationships and=
 3    T: I see [yes (.) yes
 4    C:       [and er especially with women=
 5 →  T: Yes. Well that's interesting for someone
 6       who's been married twice=
          ((laughing tone))
 7    C: = It is isn't it? .hh h[uh huh huh
 8    T:                        [.hh huh huh huh uh
 9       and has three children! Huh h[uh huh
10    C:                               [huh huh
11       ° two of which are daughters °.
```

In lines 5–6, T makes a **therapeutic intervention** in a humorous tone of voice that is at the same time an appropriate comment on the known facts. C gives an immediate response in the same tone and both participants laugh together. However, it is the client's prerogative to initiate a light-hearted approach and it is clear throughout the data that when the therapist responds in like manner this creates an ambience of warmth that makes it easier for the client to talk. The evidence for this is that the flow of the dialogue is easier when there are few or no delays in client responses.

The examples in the data reveal that clients mostly take the initiative in setting up a humorous gloss. After all, it is the client's life that is being examined. He or she has the right to choose how it is talked about. Even with a client as ready as the one in the last example to take a light-hearted approach the therapist can get it wrong as in the following:

(9) [JP/E/1]
```
 1    C: Yes but I had the Jekyll and the Hyde.
 2       When I was drunk I was one thing. And
 3       when I was sober I was another.
 4    T: Mmm
 5    C: and (.) you start to go insane cos you -
 6       you lose yer (.) you lo[se y]er own =
 7    T:                        [yes ]
 8    C: = personal[ity
 9    T:           [yes =
10    C: =You're not sure which one it is
11    T: Yes
```

```
12    C: You don't know whether it's A or B =
13 →  T: =or C or D or E or F. Hahaha
14    C: Yeah (.) The great thing about being
15       sort of sober (.) is that you keep the
16       same all the time ....
```

The implication is that whilst T's taking up the invitation to laugh is appropriate, strengthening emotional affiliation with C, when T is the one who proffers the invitation it can be rejected.[2] C gives a token acknowledgement that T has said something, but he does not respond to the joke. He carries on talking in serious vein.

The first part of this chapter is intended to give readers some idea of the types of responses that occur in conversation, and the purpose they serve. All are illustrated in the following extended extract of troubles-telling enabling readers to see the usefulness of different responses in different contexts.

Troubles-telling

I shall now take a stretch of troubles-telling and analyse the over-all organisation of the dialogue. The sequence is divided into four parts, each of which will be tracked separately for the greater ease of the reader. The focus will be on the analysis of the segments of the story and how the therapist manages her responses in order to find the underlying clues to the client's problem:

(10a) [JP/M1/11101]
```
 1 T: .hh Right Minna. So hhh you - you were
 2    telling me that you were
 3    disappointed about Christ [mas]
 4 C:                          [Yes. I'm
 5    always disappointed.
 6 T: Always?
 7 C: Oh [yes.
 8 T:    [Yes so could you give me a bit more
 9    informa[tion?
10 C:        [I was talking to someone just
11    after Christmas at a party and er (0.8)
12    and we was (.) she was saying that um (.)
13    a lot of people were disappointed about
14    Christmas. And when you think about it -
15    It's just that before Christmas - you know
16    when you see on the telly and get - (.)
17    preparing for Christmas =
```

```
18  T:  = Yes =
19  C:  = and um I just had it in my mind that it
20  T:  was going to be (.) the ideal Christ
21      [mas and all the] family's going to be =
22      [Oh  I     see  ]
23  M:  = there and we're all y'know sitting around
24      the fire [and] playing games [and] it's =
25  T:           [Yes]               [yes]
26  M:  = never like [that.
27  T:               [Hahaha I s[ee hahahahaha
28  M:                          [except that (.)
29      I (.) in my mind every year I think it's
30      going to be that w[ay a]nd so all the=
31  T:                    [ Yes]
32  M:  = people come along. My daughter came home
33      with her boy friend and his mother came because
34      she's on her own =
35  T:  = Oh I see =
36  M:  = and I said "Well bring her down" and my
37      great-uncle was there and lots of people
38      were there but um (.) then it's all over with
39      and it's just not (.) I think (.) well (.)
40      y'know a lot of pressure and spending and
41      at the end of the day people are just the
42      same as ever.
        ((laughing tone))
43  T:  Haha[hahaha
44  C:      [And I've got - my great-uncle is
45      ninety-two and he's very gropy with women
46      y'kn[ow = ((laughing tone))
47  T:      [Oh I see hahahahaha
48  C:  = this lady ca (.) and any new lady on the
49      scene y'know [he loves it] and then he =
50  T:               [Oh yes I see]
51  C:  = puts his hand on her kn[ee (.)] I could =
52  T:                           [ Yes ]
53  C:  = see her squirming and (.) very (.) um
54      tou[chy-feely
55  T:     [Yes yes.
56      Well that's the bit that bother[s you.
57  C:                                 [But
58      it - yeah. He thinks because he's
59      ninety-two he can=
60  T:  = get away with it = (( laughing tone))
61  C:  = at ninety two. So I defend the wo[men you =
62  T:                                     [Hahaha
63  C:  = [know
64  T:    [Hahaha. Has he done it all his life?
```

```
65      (0.6)
66 C:   No (.) no becau[se
67 T:              [it may be just because
68      he thinks he's licen[sed be]cause he's=
69 C:                       [ Yes ]
70 T:   ninety t[wo years old.
71 C:           [Yes (.) yes
72 T:   Oh right. Yes. So what (.) How would you like
73      Christmas to be?
```

Lines 1–9 provide the story preface, the invitation to talk. The topic 'disappointment about Christmas' has already been introduced by C in a prior utterance. In line 4, C accepts the topic and enlarges it to include all Christmases: "I'm always disappointed". T picks up on the qualifying lexical item 'always' and feeds it back to C in line 6. In line 7, C agrees that the topic is now "Christmas is always disappointing". Thus both participants are properly aligned to this topic, i.e., they agree they are talking about the same thing.

Lines 10–43 provide the background material. First C makes use of two avoidance devices, which serve to relieve her from taking personal responsibility for the feeling of disappointment. The first (line 12) is an example of the general purpose **A3N**, the **account apparently appropriate, negativer** (Sacks, 1992):[3] to wit there is no need for C to account for her disappointment over Christmas since "a lot of people were disappointed about it." The second disclaimer is related to this idea and extends over lines 18–26. C has an image of an ideal Christmas and whilst she does everything to make it so, "it's never like that". This is an example of an **extreme case formulation** (Pomerantz, 1986).[4]

In lines 36–42 C describes everything she has done to make it a good Christmas, yet she exits on a sombre note (lines 40–42) with the enigmatic statement "at the end of the day people are just the same as ever". It is the first of similar statements that need to be deciphered as one of the clues to the meaning of C's disappointment.

Lines 44–45 constitute the climax of the story: an account of the great-uncle's encounter with a guest. Whilst treating the subject lightly, C's lexical choices reveal that she is not happy with the situation: "I could see her squirming" (lines 51 and 53).

Lines 56–73 take the form of a transition stage beginning with T's intervention (line 56) "Well that's the bit that bothers you", revealing that she is also well aware of C's real feelings. Whilst T continues

to affiliate herself to C's jokey style in lines 60, 62, 64 and 70, she
returns to the topic of unpacking the meaning of C's disappointment
over Christmas in lines 72–73.

The following extract continues from where the last left off:

(10b) [JP/M1/11101]
```
72 T: Oh right. Yes. So what (.) How would you like
73    Christmas to be?
74 C: ° I don't know °
75 T: Do you get a strong sense of (.) pleasure
76    from having all the family together?=
77 C: NO! ((both laugh))
78 T: YES! (.) ° I was wondering ° that's what
79    makes it good (.) is to have the people
80    you really want around you?
81 C: No. I think I'd be better off with a bunch
82    of strangers. [Hahahahaha
83 T:              [REALLY? right (.) right. Even
84    your husband and your children?
85 C: Oh (.) with my husband and my daughter - but
86    (.) um =
87 T: But not with those others! Hahahahaha.
88 C: It's because we live in a large house and
89    we've got plenty of room and so everyone
90    assumes whenever there's a holiday um - Oh
91    we'll all go round to Minna's house (   )
92    and everyone arrives a[nd
93 T:                       [ It's a lot of work
94    then?
95 C: It is when they go - the changing the
96    sheets.
97 T: I see (.) right. So how many people were
98    there?
99 C: Um (.) Well there were only seven of us
100    for Christmas lunch and the next day all
101    our children came cos we've got eight
102    children between us and now they've all
103    got partners so that's immediately
104    sixteen [ and a ]=
105 T:         [Oh I see ]
106 C: =grandchild and it's all just spread out.
107 T: I see. You've got a very big table, have
108    you?
109 C: YEAH. But my husband loves entertaining.
110 T: Oh DOES he?
111 C: "Oh come round!" he says.
112 T: =And he's the life and soul of the party
```

```
113      is he?=
114 C:   Yes (.) yes.
115 T:   Oh (.) Right. So who does all the cooking?
116 C:   Oh he does. He loves all the cooking and
117      everything. He's brilliant.
118 T:   So he thoroughly enjoys himself?
119 C:   Yes.
120 T:   So what would you rather that you (.) you
121      could have your children and get rid
122      of these others?
123 C:   Yes (.) I'm alright for a short space of
124      time - like you say - I'm alright in a (   )
125      and then I've had enough =
126 T:   = Yes =
127 C:   = but by that time people have all had a
128      bit to drink and they're ready to - heh heh-
129      carry on round [the table
130 T:                  [Hahaha well what do they
131      do when they carry on round the table? What
132      are they actually talking about? Playing
133      games?
134 C:   Yeah. Yeah=
135 T:   = and you don't really enjoy it?
136 C:   Up to a point.
137 T:   ° Yes (.) yes °
138      (3.00)
139 C:   I just found it disappointing because (.)
140      I don't know if it was (.) I don't know if
141      it was just this year - I don't know if
142      it was because I'd been ill and I thought
143      this was going to be the ultimate Christmas
144      just - in fact I didn't think I was going
145      to be here this Christmas =
146 T:   = Oh I see (    ) Yes (.) yes.
```

Whilst this extract continues to be a story about Christmas, it is structurally different from the previous sequence (10a) in that it is led by the therapist, who initiates and establishes a **chain** of question/answer adjacency pairs. T now has enough information to play a more active role in the story-telling. T can now set about unpacking the meaning of the generalisation 'disappointing', a **metaconstruction**[5] which, in order to be understood, needs first to be analysed for its component parts.

Lines 72–93 constitute a **chain** of question and answer. The most visible feature of this sequence is that after the first open question, all the rest are closed. The initial open question gets an "I don't know" response (line 74) which could bring the talk to a standstill. "I don't know" is an answer that has been explored by Hutchby (2002) and Potter (1997) (see below). It can be a way of avoiding giving an answer. Faced with the problem of what to say next, T initiates (lines 75–76) the exploration of a sub-topical. "Do you get a strong sense of pleasure from having all the family together?", a question that asks for a simple 'yes' or 'no' response.

Yet the question, though simple, is not easy to answer, because of its implications. What happens if C says 'no'? This is exactly what she does. It is said with such force that both participants simultaneously burst into joint laughter (line 77). The interchange is playful and humorous, and T is responding in this vein by emphasising the force of C's "NO!" by an equally strong "YES!", thereby validating in a paradoxical way by using "YES!" in a way that means 'yes, your 'no' is right.' "YES!" serves as a preface to asking the same question in a different way. The affiliation built up through this 'game with words', makes it easy for C to say what she likes: to express her feelings without holding back. As a result more useful information comes to the surface enabling T to choose another sub-topic "It's a lot of work then?".

At last T has something to go on to help her to find out what the underlying disappointment is. T's questions in lines 72–93 are **warranted**, because in example (10a) C has described her 'ideal Christmas' (lines 19–24) and apparently done her best to fulfil all the requirements, yet it is still disappointing. What T is doing in these opening turns of example (10b) is challenging C's definition of an ideal Christmas, since, according to her story, it had not worked. There must be another reason for M's disappointment, so therefore T must hunt for more clues by taking up different topics and exploring them.

In lines 94–119, T explores the sub-topic "It's a lot of work then?". A new **chain** of question and answer, of a different type from the first, begins. Here is a group of factual questions that are much easier to answer because they have no emotional implications. However, this topic proves to be a blind alley. Everything C says indicates not only that Christmas is not a lot of work, but that it is a happy time.

Lines 120–146 make up the final section of this sequence. A third sub-topic is introduced in line 120 "So what would you rather that you (.) you could have your children and get rid of these others?". C's response (lines 123–129) "I'm alright for a short space of time ... and then I've had enough but by that time people have all had a bit to drink and they're ready to carry on round the table" ties back to lines 20–24 when she describes her 'ideal' Christmas as "all the family's going to be there and we're all y'know sitting round the fire and playing games".

T picks up on the anomaly by asking C if they are "playing games". C's confirmation enables T to pursue the challenge "and you don't really enjoy it?" (line 135). C's response "Up to a point" concedes only partial acceptance. After T's token response there is a pause of three seconds, that marks the end of Ts final attempt to get at the root of the problem. Neither participant gives any sign of attempting to initiate a next turn, no intakes of breath, no paralinguistic sounds.

Had C herself not opted to take the lead and initiate a **formulation** that offers a possibility for the solution of the problem things might have been different. T might have chosen to continue in her role as initiator and the ensuing sequence would have been different. After the three second pause C offers T information that opens up the exploration of a topic not previously available, C's illness. T responds with a token of surprise (line 146).

T's failure to get results in unravelling the nature of the problem could be related to the fact that T initiated the topics. There is always a risk in a service encounter that topics may be prematurely introduced when working with sensitive material that clients have not been able to face on their own. Although the search for the problem had been up to line 137 unsuccessful, affiliation and alignment had been maintained. The existence of "the deeply remedial potential of emotional reciprocity" (Jefferson & Lee, 1992, p. 546) is here reflected in C's willingness to go along with whatever T proposes, and in the spontaneity and congruence of the jointly produced laughter episodes.

T's efforts were not in vain. C takes the initiative in the section that follows:

(10c)
```
147 C:  I wanted it to be this ultimate Christmas =
148 T:  = Yes I see so because you thought it was
149     such a wonderful thing [to ] to be alive to =
150 C:                         [Yes]
151 T:  be here for Christmas therefore you
152     expected it to be sort of something
153     wonderful.
154     (.)
```

```
155 C:  Yes.
156 T:  I see - something out of the u[sual.
157 C:                               [Yes I did.
158     People are still the same though.
159 T:  Yes hahaha
```

C now offers new information "I wanted it to be this ultimate Christ-mas" (line 147). T then offers a **candidate elaboration** (lines 148–153). This is a device used by therapists to unpack the meaning of a client's statement (see Chapter Seven). The lexical item "ultimate", which is ambivalent because it can mean the last or the best, needs to be elabo-rated. T draws on what she has already gathered from the preceding talk to transform "ultimate" to something "wonderful", because C didn't think she was going to be here this Christmas (lines 148–149). C's unqualified confirmation shows her agreement with T's elabora-tion. However, once again she follows up with an enigmatic state-ment—"People are still the same though" which echoes a similar statement at the beginning of this therapy session, "at the end of the day people are just the same as ever" (lines 41–42, extract (10a)).

C opens a new sub-topic related to her illness:

(10d)
```
160 C:  My illness was never mentioned by anybody
161     [and
162 T:  [Uh huh. Would you rather it was mentioned?
163 C:  I don't know.
164 T:  You mean people ignored the fact that
165     you'd been ill? =
166 C:  = YEAH =
167 T:  = is that what you're getting at?
168 C:  YEAH. And it (.) ° I suppose that (.) they
169     didn't realise that I wanted it to be
170     that special Christmas.°
171 T:  ° What could they have done differently if
172     they'd known that?°
173 C:  Well. They couldn't have done anything
174     as they couldn't have changed. They'd
175     still have been the same people.
```

T continues to explore C's disappointment by taking up the new topic. She helps C to unpack the meaning of line 160 by initiating a ques-tion/answer sequence that incorporates three candidate elaborations followed by a hypothetical question (lines 171–172).[6] This invitation to C to imagine what people could have done differently is rejected on the grounds that "they couldn't have changed. They'd still have been the same people." (line 174): yet another comment on other people and their inability to do anything other than what they have always done.

Later on the same tape:

(10e)
```
199 T: Yes I see (.) Mm. So in a way it's because
200    Christmas was the same way it's always
201    been =
202 C: = Mm =
203 T: = and it was disappointing
204    (.)
205 C: Yes.
206 T: I think it's also something to do with
207    you've had a very difficult year.
208 C: Yes.
209 T: And not one person acknowledged =
210 T: = "Minna's had a tough time"
211 C: YES. That would have been LOVELY!
212 T: Yes. It would have been some
213    recognition - I can understand that.
214 C: Can you?
215 T: Yes (.) Yes.
```

In the final extract of this particular stretch of talk, T continues with another candidate elaboration which leads to C's strong affirmation "YES. That would have been LOVELY."

When in line 162, T asks C "Would you rather it was mentioned?" C displays doubt in her answer "I don't know". In this final extract, T once more produces a candidate elaboration which is expressed in stronger lexical terms—"And not one person acknowledged 'Minna's had a tough time' " (lines 209–210), which receives an equally strong affirmation. This demonstrates that it is worthwhile pursuing what appears to be an important clue by transforming the structure of the candidate elaboration.

Examples of three kinds of clues provided by the client

C's lexical choices and style of delivery in the first part of the sequence (10a) provide the clues for T's selection of **candidate elaborations** in the second (10b). We have analysed how T made use of the ambiguity displayed by C in her troubles-telling. Ambiguities are always worth investigating because they can reflect the structure of the underlying conflict. Another kind of clue lies in the answer 'I don't know'.

Hutchby (2002) has produced a study of how children in counselling use the lexical phrase 'I don't know', not in the cognitive sense of a knowledge disclaimer, but as a strategy for resisting the counsellor's incitement to talk. He notices an astonishingly large frequency of this particular response in his data. He finds that this response does the work of protecting the child from being drawn into talking about painful subjects connected with the parents' separation or divorce.

Whilst older children can choose to refer themselves for counselling, the younger children in Hutchby's study have usually been referred by adults. They are at a disadvantage in that they are unlikely to understand what counselling entails. If they knew in advance that the process involved talking about painful subjects they would probably not have wanted to come. Thus it is hardly surprising that they develop and make use of strategies to avoid such situations.

In the private practice of psychotherapy, where adults pay for a service, they know they will have to address sensitive issues. They know that if they resist doing so their therapy will take longer and will cost more money. It is probably for this reason that the incidence of 'I don't know' in my data is very small. However, adult clients' far greater incentive to cooperate does not mean that they do not develop resistance strategies. In psychotherapy, where clients have an all-too-understandable reluctance to reveal what is really worrying them, as in example (10) above, therapists' skills in finding indirect ways of getting relevant information are paramount. We shall take this theme further in Chapter Seven.

The particular type of 'I don't know' response analysed by Hutchby (2002) is known as 'free-standing', i.e., it is a complete turn in itself. We shall now examine another use of this utterance as it occurs twice in example (10b), lines 139–145. They are not free-standing. They serve as a preface to something else. They are of the kind 'I don't know if...':

1) I just found it disappointing because (.)
2) I don't know if it was just this year

3) I don't know if it was just because I'd been ill and I thought this was going to be the ultimate Christmas just

4) In fact I didn't think I was going to be here this Christmas.

It is now clear that (1) and (4) form a complete utterance and that (2) and (3) comprise an insert that is twice **repaired**, each correction beginning in the same way—"I don't know if" and each adding something extra. It is only in the last amendment that the topic of C's illness arises. In this small sequence the twice-repeated self-repair displays C's difficulty in bringing up the subject of her illness, a sensitive topic. We can see the purpose of this insert between the start and the end of the main utterance. It serves as a preparation and justification for C's final statement.

It seems that in this extract there is some kind of resistance taking place. C expresses strong doubt through her repetitions of "I don't know". Does she really doubt that her illness has something to do with her disappointment about Christmas? I suggest that there could be two good reasons for the structure and lexical choices of this turn. Either she may be diffident about making a contribution towards diagnosis, seeing that as the prerogative of the therapist, or she may be providing herself with a **stake inoculation** (Potter, 1997) from having to participate in the discussion of painful subjects. Perhaps, by expressing doubt about the accuracy of her opinion she hopes the therapist will discount it as of no therapeutic relevance.

The third clue is the repetition of the formulaic utterances about 'people' of which we have three examples which occur at lines 41–42, 158 and 174–175, all of which stand out because of their apparent lack of relevance to the surrounding text. They point to an underlying theme that has to do with her disappointment, which turns out to be unconnected with the event of Christmas, but is strongly related to the failure of other people to understand how she feels.

The ability of the therapist to pick appropriate topics and ask appropriate questions depends on the information provided by the client and the way that information is presented:

"Any aspect of linguistic behaviour—lexical, prosodic, phonological and syntactic choices—together with the use of particular codes, dialects or styles—may function as a contextualization cue, indicating those aspects of context which are relevant in interpreting what a speaker means." (Drew & Heritage, 1992, p. 8)

The following extract with the same client, taken from a therapy session after a two-week break, reveals a startling change in attitude, that is not uncommon when clients have had time to think about a previous session in detail. The work done in the therapy session can give clients the tools they need to consider their problem in a new light during the interval before the next session:

(11) [JP/M2]

```
 1  C:  And now (I see everything) as different (.)
 2      completely (.) as beneficial =
 3  T:  = Yes.
 4  C:  and um =
 5  T:  = Yes =
 6  C:  = even my own history when I look back - like
 7      Christmas (   ) it was just - it was so
 8      disappointing because of (   ) but once we'd
 9      worked through that (.) and got that over with
10      (.) during that next couple of weeks (.) I
11      thought of all the nice things that happened.
12  T:  Really? Did you?
13  C:  Well - well what happened I was taking my
14      Christmas cards down and there was a -
15      a picture on one of the cards of an old-
16      fashioned Christmas =
17  T:  = Yes =
18  C:  = with the tree and all the kids sitting around
19      with stockings and the fi::re and the Mum and
20      Da::d - I think she was sitting at the piano
21      and he was singing (.) hh hahaha >I said to my
22      husband< "That's the kind of Christmas I
23      wanted."
24  T:  Hahaha yes.
25  C:  Y'know that car::d y'know that car::d and -
26      it all had a glow about it [and er he ] =
27  T:                             [Yes yes yes]
28  C:  = said ( ) "The children are twenty-three
29      (    ) .hh hahaha so you see I couldn't really
30      give you that and you wouldn't wear a
31      crinoline any [way." So
32  T:                [Haha. That's right! Ha [haha
```

```
33  C:                                        [But
34      when I was - I was (.) I thought how ridiculous
35      but that's the Christmas I wan[ted (.)] =
36  T:                               [ Yes   ]
37  C:  = because ° I'd finished this treatment and I
38      thought >that's how it sh-should be< ° So then
39      I thought how - how unrealistic it was. It
40      was a nice time y'know (.) all the kids came
41      over and we all had a good laugh and did
42      all sorts of (.) So the next time >what I'm
43      saying is this< - the next time I go back and
44      you say "Oh we were talking about Christmas."
45      "Oh (.) it was BRILLIANT."
```

This is a good example of what I have called **retrospective reassessment** (see Chapter Seven). The trigger for this reassessment is the Christmas card C notices as she clears up after Christmas. It serves as a focus for everything she thought she wanted (lines 18–23). The interchange with her husband (lines 28–31) helps her to see how unrealistic her expectations were. She takes a fresh look at her experience of Christmas and comes to a different conclusion through the recognition of the degree to which she was affected by her need to have her illness recognised.

I have covered a variety of themes that occur in troubles-telling in psychotherapy and how these themes contribute to the overall organisation and the therapist's understanding of the client's story. Now I can show some of the ways in which these findings could be useful in everyday conversation.

The management of troubles-telling in everyday conversation

It is common practice for people to talk about their problems with others. Indeed, there is evidence that many people believe that therapy is not necessary if you have friends to talk to. I aim to show how the therapeutic dialogue is based on our knowledge of everyday conversation, but differs from it in several important ways. The most mutually beneficial motivation, both for therapists and clients, is when therapists have chosen their career because they are interested in helping to solve problems in living, and gain personal satisfaction from the work for two reasons. First, it is highly satisfying to be able to help another person to understand themselves better and make changes that enrich their lives and second, therapists' professional experience increases their understanding and knowledge of human nature.

They gather valuable information from troubles-telling which enables them to follow up clues and explore the underlying source of clients' pain. To do this successfully, therapists need to be able to distance themselves emotionally from the problem and treat it as an intellectual exercise in problem-solving. This is to a greater or lesser degree part of their training. Another advantage therapists have is the time limit of the therapy session. This helps them to stay focused on what is relevant to the discovery of the problem and encourage clients to do the same.

Long before I became a therapist I was drawn to other people's unhappiness and lent a willing ear to their problems. Often, they would say how much better they felt afterwards. I soon realised that this improvement was usually temporary, and made no real difference to their lives. Moreover, I often felt tired and emotionally drained afterwards because I let them go on too long. When I complained to my husband he said "More fool you for listening". I was not happy with that. None of us like to admit that our motives for 'good deeds' could be questionable, but I realised he was right. By complaining, I was doing troubles-telling myself which was not fair to him. I began to look at why I felt impelled to do something that I found upsetting.

I realised that I wanted to be seen as a kind and caring person, and my own carefully concealed and unresolved unhappiness enabled me to empathise very quickly with other unhappy people. The snag was I could not avoid feeling their pain. They would go away feeling better and I felt worse. I recognised that there is a certain arrogance in thinking we can help others. We assume that we have the power to do so. Worse, there is the danger that we may see ourselves as helpers and see those we are trying to help as helpless.

I found I could only be of real use if I got myself sorted out first. Once I had undergone a long Jungian analysis I began to understand my own inner conflicts and got to know myself better.[7] I learned that we all have to take responsibility for looking after ourselves. The task of the therapist requires the maintenance of a benevolent attitude and a calm mind, so that we can think about the problem we are dealing with in a neutral way as I hope I have demonstrated in the above transcripts. Only then was I ready to become a therapist myself.

Everyone feels better when they unburden themselves of painful feelings, but most of the time it is only a temporary relief if the underlying problem has not been addressed. Giving advice is not helpful because we cannot know what another person needs. Most of the time most people do what they want to do even though they may insist that advice is what they want. Frank Farrelly (1974) makes the point that the aim is not to help clients to feel better but to get better by encouraging them to face their fears instead of running away from them. This cannot be achieved by simply listening. Doing therapy is hard work. Listening entails giving useful feedback. Great concentration is necessary in order to take in most of what clients are saying and to give helpful responses.

To sum up, I believe that my findings about how to manage troubles-telling in psychotherapy could be helpful for those of us who wish to be of use to others by hearing them talk about their difficulties. The following list is not exhaustive but it offers suggestions for how we can handle this situation in everyday talk:

- Listen only if you want to, not because you feel you ought to. We cannot listen properly if we are in a state of worry about our own inner conflicts.
- Find a place where you can talk privately: preferably sitting-down with a cup of coffee (or other non-alcoholic drink). Agree a specific time limit and stick to it. When people are deeply distressed they will talk at great length, with no thought of your well-being.
- Use the type of responses I have described in this chapter, except for the interventions that require professional knowledge.
- Avoid giving advice except when you are invited to do so. Even then we need to proceed with caution, because you cannot know what others want. If your advice is taken and it goes wrong, you will get the blame.
- Avoid over-dosing on sympathy. Keep the atmosphere as light-hearted as possible.
- Avoid making judgements. Avoid collusion with others' distorted thinking. Never join in blaming. You do not know the real situation. You cannot know anything about a non-present person, and

if that person is identified by the troubles-teller as the cause of the trouble, never accept this as reliable evidence.

- Ask questions to clarify anything you do not understand.
- Keep your focus on the person you are talking with, not on your own reactions to what they are saying. Stay neutral and bring the talk to a stop yourself.
- If the troubles-teller is a member of your own family, proceed with caution. All the above points need to be even more strictly observed, because of the greater difficulty of getting too emotionally involved. Do not fall into the trap of thinking you know what is good for them. Telling them what to do is counter-productive. Help them to find out for themselves. Respect their autonomy by encouraging them to unpack the meaning of their utterances.

Conclusion

My intention in writing this chapter was to give readers some idea of the uses of troubles-telling in psychotherapy: how therapists guide their clients by giving them good quality feedback and by making appropriately placed interventions. Of primary importance is the maintenance of alignment and affiliation. The first is a more cerebral and neutral activity that requires attention to the search for meaning through the pursuit of the relevance of the dialogue to clients' problems. The second addresses the need to create a warm, responsive atmosphere to support and encourage clients as they struggle to understand what they are doing in their lives that prevents them from recognizing their own needs and doing their best to satisfy them.

In the next chapter I shall explore the third and final stage of therapy, when clients have begun to take on board the nature of therapy talk and work on equal terms with their therapists. Once this begins to happen, there is a profound change in the character of the therapeutic dialogue.

NOTES

1. Collusion is the enemy of good therapeutic practice. In many cases, the source of clients' problems arises through a certain degree of self-delusion which comes from the desire to avoid the pain of coming to terms with reality. One of the great arts of good practice

involves the resolution of a paradox, the meshing of the maintenance of an empathic relationship with a refusal to agree with clients' initial assessments of their situation, especially if it involves
blaming external agencies.

2. A joke by the therapist that falls flat because it elicits no response
from the client does not help the flow of the dialogue. A fragile
sense of personal worth is one of the most common features of help-
seeking clients. They can easily be offended by what they see as
a display of superior understanding. Milton Erickson, one of the
great psychotherapists, laid down a sensible rule for this situation:
never try to be one up with your client, aim to be one down.

3. The general purpose A3N proposed by Sacks (1992) is a device that
people use to avoid explaining what they mean. They make excuses
for their own behaviour by using such phrases as 'everyone does it,
don't they?' This device is quickly picked up by children. Instead
of giving a sound reason why they should be allowed to do something, they may say 'Everyone else's mother lets them do this, so
why can't I?'.

4. Hutchby & Wooffitt (1998) summarize what Pomerantz (1986) calls
extreme case formulations. These are devices that "invoke an object
or event's maximal and minimal properties". (Hutchby & Woofitt,
1998, p. 209–212) 'Never' is an example of such an extreme. C dis-
counts the possibility of ever being able to see Christmas as anything but disappointing.

5. A **metaconstruction**, a term used in neuro-linguistic programming,
is the same kind of thing as Wowk's (1989) **polyglot categories** (see
Chapter Seven). To get at the meaning it is necessary to unpack the
term, to break it down into its components, as the speaker understands them.

6. The usefulness of hypothetical questions in psychotherapy was discovered by Perakyla (1995). They invite clients to use their imagination to look at situations from a fresh angle.

7. I do not wish to imply that any of us ever completes the task of self-
understanding. It is a life-long task. However, I believe it is very
important that therapists should remember that, however much we
have been dedicated to discovering ourselves, we are not automa-
tons or saints. We can still surprise ourselves by our own actions.
Since therapists are guides we have a responsibility to know as
much as we can about ourselves before we take on the task of helping others to do the same.

CHAPTER SEVEN

The identification of the client's problem

Chapter Five showed how therapists encourage clients to begin to tell their stories. In Chapter Six we looked at clients' troubles-telling: how therapists contribute to the production of the stories by giving feedback with appropriate responses, and identifying clues that point to the underlying problem. I have described some of the ways in which we can apply the principles of the findings to improve our skills in everyday conversation. This chapter is concerned with the third stage of therapy talk which only happens once the first two are well advanced. We shall explore those elements of therapists' and clients' contributions that work towards the identification of clients' problems. This is the most rewarding stage of the process for therapists, because they can see how clients are beginning to use language in a new way to work things out for themselves.

As clients absorb the therapeutic process through the therapist's example the character of the dialogue begins to change. Clients make a greater contribution because they have learned how to do therapy talk through a process of osmosis. Therapists continue to give support with appropriate responses and relevant interventions, but now clients no longer do troubles-telling, their stories incorporate a new ability to unpack meanings and see connections between past and present behaviour by applying the principles they have unconsciously absorbed through practice. The efforts of both participants in working for the clarification of the problem creates a structure which incorporates a type of cooperative talk-in-interaction that accelerates the therapeutic process.

All the sections in this chapter are governed by two requirements that drive the therapeutic task. First, the establishment of participant alignment and affiliation and second, the unpacking of the meaning of particular lexical items used by clients. Because of the ambiguity of words there is an ongoing need to monitor two factors: the understanding of what is going on in the talk itself, and the progress that is being made in the identification of the problem. In my data the initiation of these elements comprises a vital part of the therapist's activity.

First, I acknowledge my indebtedness to Wowk's (1989, 1995) recognition of the importance of how emotions are dealt with in therapy. Wowk's argument is that the domain of emotions has been disregarded by sociology. Emotions have been treated as a **polyglot category**. Therefore lexical items such as 'worried' and 'depressed' need to be unpacked in order to discover the meaning those terms have for the client in a certain context.

Wowk (1989) proposes that a disadvantage of generalisations, "open-ended terms with a variety of possible situated senses" (Wowk, 1989, p. 58), is that they conceal the underlying meaning. Garfinkel and Sacks (1970) refer to such generalisations as glosses. However, the term gloss does not only apply to individual lexical units. It can constitute a "masking or covering-up of 'what really happened'" (Jefferson, 1986, p. 435). For example in Chapter Six, example 10, apparently about disappointment with Christmas, there is an underlying disappointment of a different kind (see Appendix 2:1). Edwards & Potter (1992) prioritise two factors to be taken into account for the analysis of description, first, "the **rhetorical** context of the events" and second, "the processes of event reconstruction occurring over time" (Edwards & Potter, 1992, p. 55). This is the process I have called retrospective **reassessment**. It will be discussed in this chapter.

Wowk draws on Garfinkel's (1967) model for the unpacking of what he called "individual documentary evidences", i.e., the actual lexical items used by the person-with-the-problem to describe their feelings, to discover a "presupposed underlying pattern". Translated in terms of this study, this means that the way clients describe their personal experiences and feelings provides lexical cues—documentary evidences—that enable therapists to make use of certain devices to make possible the unpacking of the meaning of indexical terms used by clients. These devices are the subject of this chapter and include therapists' interventions, **clients' elaborations**, and the **joint production** of what Wowk (1989) terms mutual elaboration. Although this is a mutual task I use the name **collaborative elaboration** to make the point that, although the focus is on the client's problem, each participant plays a complementary part.

The term **candidate elaboration** is so called because it is a candidate for the client's attention. It serves the purpose of helping clients to unpack the meaning of their own utterances by suggestions about what that meaning might be. They are suggestions, based on prior turns, and the final **decision** rests with clients, who, by virtue of their 'inside' knowledge of themselves can judge if the elaboration is true for them or not. The term elaboration used alone refers to those detailed unpackings of their feelings or experiences that clients do for themselves; a form of self-therapy.[1] The task of therapists is to facilitate clients so that they can actively participate. It is not the job of the therapist to tell the clients whether they are right or wrong about their own feelings. An essential element of therapists' skills resides in the provision of a comfortable, non-coercive setting to help clients to recognise the true nature of these underlying feelings. A primary requirement for candidate elaborations is that they should be **warranted**: i.e., they need to be related to what has been said before.

As clients become more aware of their emotional responses, instead of accepting or rejecting the candidate elaboration, they discover they have enough knowledge about themselves to be able to make the choice of partial acceptance. They can respond with an elaboration of their own. Therapists may then either confirm clients' statements or go on to make a further candidate elaboration, which, in turn, may result in the client producing another. Thus a chain of elaborations conducted by both participants may be set in motion to be resolved when consensus has been achieved. This process, **collaborative elaboration**, is particularly important for this study because it is strongly pervasive in the final-stage work of defining a client's problem, as we shall see later in this chapter. This feature can only come into being when there exists a strong sense of affiliation between the participants, and of trust on the part of clients.

Jefferson (1986) identifies the need for "achieving an environment for unpacking" (Jefferson, 1986, p. 438–439). She proposes that there can be a preparation for an unpacking, a "pre-affiliation" where the recipient introduces laughter, for example, as a form of encouragement for first speakers to explicate a disclosure in greater detail.

Summaries and formulations

Coherence in conversation is maintained by the participants making sense of each other's utterances in order to clear up misunderstandings on-the-spot. The term **formulation** covers a range of devices the purpose of which is "to enable co-participants to settle on one of many possible interpretations of what they have been saying" (Heritage & Watson, 1979, p. 123).

In psychotherapy, **formulations** serve a dual purpose. First, as in ordinary conversation, they are used to summarise the gist of prior talk. Second, as a result of the needs of the task of therapy, they are used in a number of ways that have to do with therapists bringing clients' attention to what is going on in the work of searching for a solution to clients' problems.

In the first case, therapists remind clients of information they have given, not in immediately prior turns, but some time earlier in that session or a previous one. In the second, therapists produce interpretations that summarise 'how-the-task-of-therapy-is-progressing' by making candidate elaborations that offer new connections between different aspects of what-is-already-known. Such connections are candidate unpackings of the underlying problem designed for clients' attention. How these devices work will be explicated in this section of the chapter.

According to Heritage & Watson (1979), all talk is **indexical**, including formulations. There can be no definitive meaning, since all lexical items are ambiguous. Thus any formulation constrains the coparticipant to respond by acceptance, partial acceptance or rejection of the proposition. The authors thereby conclude that a formulation and its recipiency constitute an adjacency pair: the recipient being under a constraint to confirm or disconfirm the particular interpretation offered by the formulator. The following example illustrates a therapist's formulation (indicated by F) of a client's stretch of prior talk and its confirmation (D+) or disconfirmation (D–) by the client. The cipher 'D' stands for **decision**:

(1) [JP/Ed3]
```
1   C:  ... But there's some (.) part of me thinks
2       (.) it's a good idea because I'm - I'm delaying
3       gratification which seems to be a mature thing
        ((laughs))
4   T:  Yes =
5   C:  = Huh =
6   T:  = Oh I SEE. Right.
7   C:  Y'know I'm thinking that the—the other things
8       are competing in me. One is that "Oh yes, it's
9       mature. I believe it is mature to delay gra-
10      gratification. The spiritual side of me says
11      "But I want to live in the day". Then =
12 F→ T:  = Yes. Oh I SEE so you're interpreting wanting
13      to live in the day in a certain way. Right
14      (.)
15 D+→ C: Um (.) Yes (.) Yes (.) I mean it's wanting to
16      live in the day I'm (    ) in that I want more
17      freedom ...
```

This formulation constitutes a "transformation or paraphrase of some prior utterance" (Heritage & Watson, 1979, p. 129). T preserves C's prior statement "I want to live in the day" (line 11) and modifies it with "in a certain way" (line 13), a suggestion that invites a response. This works as a candidate elaboration since C's uptake both confirms the elaboration and initiates the unpacking of what "living in the day" means to him, "I want more freedom": a preface to the unpacking of what he wishes to do with his time.

The following extract illustrates a related type of formulation called **upshot** (Heritage & Watson, 1979). This differs from example (1) in that, rather than being a summary, it suggests a pre-supposition. In this case the formulation is disconfirmed:

(2) [JP/L2]
```
1   C:  No I worked with her after I'd finished.
3   T:  Oh I see.
4   C:  So er (.) it was in the (.) um it was in the
5       morn =
```

```
6    T:  = Yes.
7    C:  Well it was at the end of the morning while
8        I carried on doing =
9  U→ T:  = so you would rather have gone home. You'd
10        rather not have worked with her.
11 D→ C:  Um (2.0) No I can't say that.
12    T:  Uh huh
13        (7.0)
14    C:  She wasn't a kid (.) a kid I got a lot of en-
          joyment
15        out of her personality.
```

Upshots are different from formulations in that they "presuppose some unexplicated version of gist" (Heritage & Watson, 1979, p. 132). Unlike example (1) where the formulation is warranted by C's prior talk, T has taken a prior statement by C that she would rather have gone home to mean that she did not want to work with the child, an unwarranted assumption.[2]

Pomerantz (1984a) analyses the way that confirmations and disconfirmations differ in their effect on **procedural consequentiality**. Confirmations are preferred and therefore they are not problematic. However, disconfirmations are problematic because in mundane conversation people see disagreement with a participant to be a threat to their right to their own opinions. Hence, as Pomerantz has shown, disconfirmation is often preceded by agreement as a way of preparing for disagreement by mitigating its effect.

In this example the difficulty in responding is illustrated by an overlong pause of 7 seconds after C's disconfirmation. The proof of C's willingness to cooperate, despite the disruptive effect of the disagreement, lies in her uptake in line 14 when she transforms T's statement that "you'd rather not have worked with her" (lines 9–10), which attributes the cause to C's attitude to the child: to other-attribution—that the fault lies with the child for not being enjoyable to work with.

The contrast between these two examples demonstrates the mileage gained, in terms of encouraging clients to cooperate, by avoiding **upshots** of the kind described in example (2) and adhering to a formulation warranted by prior information from the client (example (1)). I shall now give examples of another type of therapists' intervention.

Interpretations incorporating linkages between past and present

Linkages between past and present are pervasive throughout my data. This is hardly surprising since one way that clients can become aware of changes is by comparing how they behaved in the past with their present behaviour in similar situations. Most of the time, especially in the earlier stages of therapy, it is therapists that initiate this activity. This serves to help clients to recognise that changes have taken place.[3]

The following two examples illustrate a type of formulation where therapists remind clients of information already given some time before. The formulations also do the work of candidate elaborations. They are inserted after C has concluded an extended turn:

(3) [JP/M4]
```
 1    C: I sold myself down the river because I
 2       (.)
 3    T: Yes
 4    C: I lost myself really huh [huh
 5 F→ T:                          [Huh s[o you're
 6       certainly finding yourself now [huhhuhhuh
 7                                       [Ye - ha [ha
 8    C: [ha
 9 F→ T: [hahaha and I think you started to find
10       yourself when you walked out of the house
11       with as you said a pair of knickers in your
12       handbag [and you ] =
13    C:         [Yes ye:s]
14 F→ T: = just knew you weren't going back. I think
15       that's when you finally decided in your head
16       what you wanted.
17 D+→C: Yes.
```

Here, C concludes an extended elaboration about childhood difficulties with a summary in which she blames herself for having "sold myself down the river" (lines 1 and 4). In lines 5–16, T makes a formulation in the form of a summary to remind C of a previous event that demonstrates her having taken control of her own life. C gives immediate confirmation of T's interventions in lines 7–8, 13 and 17.

(4) [JP/Ed3]
```
 1    C: Haha I'm terribly impatient. I hadn't noticed
 2       it before. No =
 3    T: = No =
```

```
4      C: A[nd
5  F→ T:     [you've not had the opportunity to notice it
6              before because you've never had such a calm
7              period before.
8              (1.8)
9  D+→C: Ah:; Yes (.) yes (.) it's true ......
```

This extract is similar to (3) in that it begins with a client's self-interpretation. By using the lexical item "terribly" as a description of "impatient" (line 1) C implies that this is not something he is happy about. T interrupts C in line 5 and transforms this realisation by focusing on the positive aspect of it (lines 5–7). The work done by this intervention offers C an accounting for not having noticed his impatience before, he has "never had such a calm period before". C has created this calm time for himself as a result of making changes in his way of life before he came for therapy (this information is available to the therapist/researcher from previous disclosures by C). C's uptake with a **change-of-state token** of surprise 'Ah' (Heritage, 1984), displays that he had not made this connection, and confirms it.

Both these extracts are instances of a therapist's intervention successfully transforming a client's downbeat assessment into a more positive one. In example (3) T was able to do this because she remembered what C said before and brought that memory back into focus for C. In example (4) T indirectly encourages C by giving him credit for providing himself with a calm environment with time to reflect and come to new understandings about himself. Thus this type of intervention, which constitutes a reframing of a client's self-derogatory realisation into a more hopeful one is strongly affiliative.

Both examples (3) and (4) display the use of the formulation/candidate elaboration. The device constitutes the first part of an adjacency pair, constraining the recipient to confirm or disconfirm the proposition.

The next example is different in kind. It opens with a conclusion/decision after a troubles-telling by C:

(5) [JP/Ma2/11598] Extract from Appendix 2:3
```
55     C: ... I'm not going to play cricket
56         any more I'm going to try something
57         different
58 F→ T: Oh Right. Well that's goo:d. - then that
59         just show:s doesn't it that you-you're
60         becoming more and more aware of what you
61         wa:nt and you're realising a lot of
```

```
62          things you've done are the sleepwalking
63          things without really thinking what you want
64          or you don't want =
65 D→ C:    = but then it's probably because I'm more
66          aware of what I don't want. But then I - I
67          guess that that's part [of it
68     T:                          [Right. Oh it is.
```

T's uptake (lines 58–64) of C's decision (lines 55–67) constitutes a confirming response, a candidate elaboration, an interpretation of how C is changing, by taking the implications of what C has said and comparing C's past with present to highlight the change. This offers C the proposition that his decision constitutes a major change. However, T's candidate elaboration is partially accepted by C: "more aware of what I don't want" (lines 65–66). He mitigates what could be seen as a rejection of T's offering by proffering a partial agreement in lines 65–67.

All three interventions are situated after a client's troubles-telling ending with a client's self-realisation. In each case the vehicle for the link between past and present is a candidate elaboration, which is agreed or partially agreed by the recipient.

We now move on to another kind of **therapeutic intervention**.

Therapist's self-disclosure and information

In Chapter Five (examples (6) and (7)) I have already described situations where the therapist says something about her own experience to help the client to start talking. In the following example I shall show how therapists' self-disclosure can help clients to remember their own experience and then begin to unpack the meaning of those experiences.[4] In some cases therapists give unrequested information to clients. In example (6) self-disclosure and information are combined. The sequence takes place after an extended stretch of dialogue that is available in Appendix 2:2. Readers may find it helpful to read the whole sequence first since it helps to explicate why T makes her intervention at this particular place:

(6) [JP/Ed2b/2829]
```
1  C:   ... intellectually (.) I think (.)
2       I can understand it =
3  T:   = I know. It's emotionally (.) grasping
4       things emotionally is much harder
5       (.)
```

```
 6 C: Yes
 7 T: =it's like you can see what other people are
 8    doing (.) I mean we all do this. I say things
 9    sometimes to my clients and afterwards I
10    think "I said that with great confidence but
11    (.) do I really do it myself?" No I don't (.)
12    for some reason =
13 C: = No =
14 T: =I say "Don't take any notice of others. What
15    does their opinion matter?" Lo and behold
16    what happens? Somebody says something and
17    I've got a bit bothered by it and I think
18    "Haven't I got out of that yet?" Ha.°well
19    y'know we go on working on these things
20    throughout our lives°.
21 C: I can certainly see the other men that I
22    know have been learning (    ) recovery_ (.)
23    they will be attracted to (.) needy (.) women
24    [and] often women with a (.) like you [say] =
25 T:    [Yes]                                 [Yes]
26 C: = sort of (.) sort of like er .hhh all things
27    being equal they y'know the (.) the guy'll be
28    attracted to somebody who's much less
29    intelligent so he can control things (.)
30 T: Oh absolutely
31 C: frightened he can't stand up to somebody of his own
32    ilk =
33 T: = yes exactly (.) control (.) that's what it's
34    all about.
35 C: Yes
36 T: If you [um
37 C:        [Well they can't get it (.) it's
38    absolutely a disaster (.) because even the weak
39    woman will get it in the end from the guy if
40    he's weak (.) [y'know li]ke me (.) Hahaha and =
41 T:              [Ye::::::;]
42 C: = that's a scene for disaster [(    ) you] hear =
43 T:                               [Absolutely]
44 C: = story after story recently on this same theme
45    I think I haven't (.) y'know I can praise myself
46    that I haven't fallen into it recently y'know
47    (.) I've been tempted to but I've backed off
48    at the last minute
```

T combines disclosure of her own experiences within a framework of information based not on her professional training, but as 'someone who has had similar experiences'. This device constitutes a display of affiliation with C which serves to encourage him to continue exploring his problem (lines 21–48).

T makes a formulaic statement that whatever we know intellectually is much harder to put into practice. C's uptake in line 21, "I can certainly see the other men ..." ties up with T's utterance in lines 7–8, "It's like you can see what other people are doing", displaying that he is aligning himself with T's description of her own problem in this area.

Thus self-disclosure can be a source of several therapeutic actions. It can demonstrate to the client that he is not alone with his problem, it can give him the confidence to discuss sensitive issues more easily and it can reinforce the affiliation between the participants.

Collaborative elaboration

(7) [JP/Ma/11598] Extract from Appendix 2:3

```
 78 C: ... YEAH (.) Yes [.hhh
 79 T:                 [Yes.
 80    That's fine. It's just exactly what you said
 81    in the supermarket. The same thing. You see?
 82    (.)
 83 C: Which one's that? Sorry? (   ) =
 84 T: = the last time on the tape. What you said is
 85    almost identical. "What am I doing here?"
 86    ((laughing tone)) y'know haha - you don't
 87    really want to be there doing the shopping
 88    Right?
 89 M: Right.
 90 T: You grab something and then you go away with
 91    the minimum because you make yourself =
 92 M: = Mm =
 93 T: = but that seems to intimate that you're not
 94    too keen on doing shopping.
 95    (1.2)
 96 C: Mm - mm (2.7) .hhh WE:LL (.) I don't think
 97    that means that I (.) don't (.) like shopping
 98    deep down - as my actual feeling [(.) I m]ean =
 99 T:                                  [Ah: I see]
100 C: = I think it's different
101    (.)
102 T: Oh (.) right =
103 C: It's more to do with being um - led
104    by (.) a sense of ought rather than want
       (this is followed by an extended elaboration)
```

T's opening candidate elaboration links two events in C's life. However lines 80–81 are ambiguous. C asks T for clarification. T gives an extended **elaboration** in lines 84–88, 90–91 and 93–94 to unpack her own meaning, a case of self-repair to fill in missing details. C's first two responses (lines 89 and 92) are confirmative. However, in line 96 he begins to give his own interpretation of the difference between the two events. He prefaces this **elaboration** with a tentative agreement before going on to disconfirm T's interpretation: an example of Pomerantz's (1984a) finding that dispreferred second assessments are often prefaced by a mitigating agreement.

Since direct disagreement is avoided as far as possible in ordinary conversation, it is hardly surprising that clients find it difficult to disagree with therapists, who are the ones who 'know what they are doing'. Therefore when this happens it is a sign that a sufficiently affiliative and non-threatening environment has been established in which clients feel they can say what they wish.

(8) [JP/Ed2b/2829] An extract from Appendix 2:2
```
189 C:  ... (3.0) hhh. Well I'm frightened
190     that I'm delaying it on pur-y'know - the fear
191     is that (.) I'm delaying it on purpose.
192     (.)
193 T: And if you delay it what might happen? What
194     is this really about? (1.9) if you delay
195     it what would happen?
196 C: Uhh (.) Well I've failed you see.
197 T: Yes. What would failing mean? (.) What would
198     actually happen? I mean in real terms?
199 C: Well I'd give in (.) well I wouldn't have a
200     relationship.
201 T: Yes. That's right.
202     (.)
203 C: Yes.
204 T: If you don't have one quickly you won't have
205     one at all.
206 C: Haha[haha
207 T:     [Hahaha[hahahahah. RIGHT. Haha[hahahahaha
208 C:            [Hahahahahahahahahahahahahah not the
209     way you let me plough on! Haha[hahahaha
210 T:                                 [HAHAHAHAhaha
211 C: Yes that's it.
212 T: Yes?
213 C: That's right.
```

T's first two candidate elaborations (lines 193–195 and 197–198) are in question form. Thus there is a particularly strong constraint on C to answer. Considering that this is a particularly difficult topic for C and related to the core of his underlying problem (verified by the length of therapy time that has been devoted to it, as C himself recognises in lines 208–209). C's willingness to play an active part in the unpacking of his underlying conflict displays that, like the client in example (7) he feels sufficiently comfortable with the therapist to do so.

T neatly sums up the nature of the problem in a one-liner (lines 204–205). It's brevity and forceful lexical choices have the impact of a joke. C's laughing uptake shows that he sees it as such. This results in an outburst of joint laughter that converges with the mutual recognition that the nature of the conflict has been solved. Just as Jefferson & Lee (1992) showed us how laughter can be used to make difficult topics easier to handle, so in this example, the final acceptance of what could be a bitter truth, is softened by the recognition that we do not have to take ourselves too seriously.

The sequential difference between examples (7) and (8) is that in (7) the **collaborative elaboration** sequence serves as a preface for an extended piece of self-analysis by C, whereas in (8), it works as a joint resolution of the underlying conflict following after a client's multi-turn **elaboration**/self-therapy.

The obstacles to the unpacking of these kinds of conflicts are great. The human attempt to try to live up to some idealised 'norm' in order to 'fit in' with society and be accepted by others gets in the way. Resistance is a Freudian (1940) concept for clients' strategies to avoid facing making changes in their lives. Leaving behind cherished illusions can seem too high a price to pay. Part of the difficulty is not knowing how such changes will affect our future. We know that clients are overcoming these obstacles when they begin to play an active part in their own therapy and make use of the skills they have learned through being involved in the process. The final section shows how, in the data, in the later stages of therapy, clients manage to work things out for themselves with minimal help from therapists.

Clients' elaborations

Clients' elaborations displaying change recognition

There are examples in the data corpus where clients make new discoveries with astonishing speed. This type of sudden recognition
has been called the **Eureka! factor**[5]:

(9) [JP/EdB]
```
1 T: Well tell me about what you were going to
2    say. It sounds so fascinating about some
3    feelings that you haven't explored or=
4    [ (   )
5 C: [ I (.) realised that I hadn't (.)
6    = experimented with a lot of feelings.
```
(C begins an extended elaboration that comprises an
unpacking of this realisation)

In this example the opening three lines display that T has taken up
a new topic mentioned by C in a prior turn, and transformed it into
an invitation to talk. C's uptake, constitutes a new realisation about
himself, and this leads to an extended sequence of self-exploration.
The following occurs at the beginning of a consultation:

(10) [JP/M3]
```
1  T: Minna. How have you been since last time you
2     ca[me?
3  M:   [Okay. Yes -seems a long time ago
4     actu[ally
5  T:     [It does seem a long time doesn't
6     i[t? Wh]at is it - two weeks isn't it? =
7  M: [Yes]
8     = Yes it's only two weeks
9     (.)
10 T: Yes
11 M: in fact I've done a lot of reading and I've
12    done a lot of (1.7) I dunno really everything
13    just seems (.) to have been (.) easier.
```

T (line 1) opens by asking for feedback on M's state of mind
since the previous session. Instead of answering directly, M
introduces a new topic, the time factor (line 3). T specifies the
time length, "two weeks" since the previous session, bringing
the significance of the time factor to M's attention. M's repetition
of "two weeks" is preceded by the lexical item "only". She then

goes on (lines 11–13), to give an account of her activities during that period of time. The relevance of this new topic is implicit in the last three lines. M has done "a lot of reading", has found it "easier". Her perceptions about how she has experienced reading in a different way is the topic of an extended turn that follows this extract.

The hesitant style of her delivery gives the sense of her striving towards some new realisations about herself. She realises that something different is happening, but is uncertain about what is going on.

In the next example, a client who has been self-employed most of his life is feeling a sense of frustration because he has been obliged to take a temporary job beneath his capabilities in order to survive. After a few sessions of therapy he is beginning to realise that his situation has allowed him the chance to make fresh discoveries about himself:

(11) [JP/Ed]
```
 1 C: On (.) on the other hand I mean (.) I find it um
 2    (2.4) settling (.) because I know what I'm doing
 3    each morning. I know for five days. So I am
 4    finding it settling and I am finding the routine
 5    (2.0) much more (    ) some good points and some
 6    bad points y'know (    ) the bad point is my
 7    impatience    =
 8 T: = Huh huh [huh
 9 C:           [Huh huh I'm terribly impatient. I hadn't
10    noticed it before. No =
11 T: = No =
12 C: = And =
13 T: = You've not had the opportunity to notice it
14    because you've never had such a calm period before
15    (1.8)
16 C: Ah: Yes (.) yes (.) it's true (.) yes because when
17    I am (.) before when I was impatient I would just
18    sort of rush off and start something new
     (laughing tone)
19    [or
20 T: [Ha ha ha [ha ha
21 C:           [get a new job.
```

Note how the affiliative laughter shared with the therapist enhances the flow of the jointly produced talk, encouraging the client to speak spontaneously.

Clients' elaborations incorporating retrospective reassessment

I use the term **retrospective reassessment** to refer to that strategy, highly pervasive in the data, where clients show their awareness of changes by comparing past situations and/or behaviour with present ones. In the following extract the reassessment is triggered by a **Eureka!** experience. In each case, a reaction to a situation in the external world brings a sudden awareness of internal change:

```
(12) [JP/Ma/4598]
 1  C:  =I was just like trying to work (.) against
 2      the situ-haha-ation I suppose [(.)] or work =
 3  T:                                 [Yes]
 4  C:  = with it (1.2) um (1.4) and it was just clear
 5      to me that these people were fundamentally
 6      like that and they - they were not gonna
 7      change and they-they were flawed in that
 8      respect [(.)and]that y'know I'd been sort of=
 9  T:          [Mm mm ]
10  C:  =suffering because of it a [nd ]it was simply=
11  T:                             [Yes]
12  C:  =they- they thought they were brilliant
13      blokes - they -they- they were such a
14      bunch of asses really=
15  T:  = Yes so you didn't actually see that
16      when you were in the situation at school
17  C:  NO [NO - a]nd then um having to come back=
18  T:     [NO. Right]
19  C:  =with sort of so a different sort of point of
20      view...
            (in line 17—"having to come back" refers to C returning from a very
            different experience of people in America)
```

This extended elaboration and assessment of a past situation displays a major change in how C sees the situation in the present. He describes strategies that he used in the past to cope with the situation in lines 1–2 when he was trying to resolve it by trying to work with it or against it. In lines 4–8 he moves accountability for his suffering away from himself, for not being able to cope with the situation and repositions it on his classmates, for not being able to change. The catalyst that led this client to seek therapy was his experience of behaving very differently with his friends in America. On returning home, he found the old inhibitions were holding him back. This convinced him that if he could change how he interacted with other people in a different culture, then he could learn to do so in his own country. He sought out therapy to fulfil this purpose.

T's intervention (lines 15–16) constitutes a **marker** and a reinforcement of the fact that this is a new assessment. He can see it now but he could not see it then.

(13) Later in the same session:
```
 1 T: So then - how long
 2    were you in America now? One month?
 3 C: One month - three weeks actu[ally
 4 T:                              [Ha ha. So it's
 5    cha- huh huh -nged[ a bit
 6 C:                   [ three weeks haha.
 7    Yes.
 8 T: Yes yes. So then it's just so we what [this
 9 C:                                       [that's
10    amazing isn't it? Three weeks! (.) It
11    didn't strike -I just didn't think about that
12    before =
13 T: =Yes hahaha. Three weeks and a lifetime's
14    perception for change [Haha hahahahaha haha
15 C:                       [Yes. It's absolutely
16    incredible...
```

By asking C a specifying question in lines 1–2, T focuses on the time factor. She displays her surprise that it is even less than she thought by laughing (lines 4–5). C treats the laughter as an invitation to join in (line 6).

The effect of the shared laughter here does the work that we have seen it do before, that of increasing affiliation between the participants (see Chapter Six, example (10)). However, the reason for the laughter is different. In example (10) the laughter is initiated by the client as a way of making light of her problem. Here, the laughter is initiated by the therapist (lines 4–5) as a token of surprise (Heritage, 1984) at her sudden awareness of the importance of the time factor which anticipates C's sudden realisation of the connection (lines 9–12). This is the same thing that happens in ordinary conversation when someone, in an instant, sees a joke: the **Eureka! factor**.

The final interpretation of the relevance of the time factor—that big changes can happen in a short space of time—is made by T in lines 13–14. This time C does not join in the laughter. His lexical choices (lines 15–16) suggest that he is bowled over by a different emotion, a sense of wonder at this revelation.

In the prior extract, although C finally makes the realisation for himself, it is T who makes the first connection that helps him to get going.

The next extract occurs soon after the beginning of a consultation:

(14) [JP/Ma/11598] Extract from Appendix 2:3

```
40 C:  ...I've always thought that - that I
41     love cricket [(.) b]ut I was standing there and =
42 T:             [ Yes ]
43 C:  = it was a lovely day .hh and I was standing
44     there in the field - and I was thinking "What
45     THE BLOODY HELL am I doing HERE [AGAIN".HH ] =
46 T:                                  [Heh heh heh]
47 C:  = haha it's BOR[ING and I]'m not doing =
48 T:                 [.hh haha ]
49 C:  = anyth[ing I just] stood there =
50 T:         [.hh hahaha]
51 C:  = about eight hours and the ball came to me
52     about once! And I was thinking ".hh God"
53     y'know (1.2) "What am I doing here?" y'know
54     (0.8) "I just don't like it." And er - so the
55     result is I'm not going to play cricket
56     any more! I'm going to try something
57     different =
58 T:  = Oh right. Well that's goo:d - then that
59     just show:s doesn't it that you - you're
60     becoming more and more aware of what you
61     wa:nt and you're realising that lots of
62     the things you've done are the sleepwalking
63     things without really thinking what you want
64     or you don't want =
65 C:  = but then it's probably because I'm more
66     aware of what I don't want. But then I - I
67     guess that that's part of it.
```

This is another example of an instant realisation. Something C thought he had always loved suddenly seems abhorrent, as displayed in the increased volume of his voice and his strong lexical choices. T's response (lines 58–64) comprises both a summary/formulation of how one change can be extrapolated to other areas of his life. He feels he "isn't doing anything" (lines 47 and 49). He asks "What am I doing here?" (line 53), a recognition that he has passively done things without thinking whether he really wants to do them or not. He makes an instant decision to "try something different" (lines 56–57).

(15) Later on in the same tape: extract from Appendix 2:3

```
102 T: = Oh (.) right =
103 C: = I think it's more to do with being um (.) led
104    by (.) a sense of ought rather than
105    want [ (.) because] certainly when I was in =
106 T:       [Oh yes I see]
107 C: = y'know that state a few weeks ago where
108    y'know I was (.) really calm and
109    (.)
110 T: Yes
111 C: In a state of relaxed concentration and I was
112    doing what I wanted to do.
113    (.)
114 T: Right
115 C: then it was great and I - shopping was
116    interesting - but y'know - lots of (.)
117    >YEAH: THAT's a succinct way of putting it<
118    (.) the time when I didn't want to be there =
119 T: Yes
120 C: because my way of thinking (.) was
121    setting myself up for a fall =
122 T: = Yes. Setting yourself up for a fall =
123 C: = whereas - whereas - whereas - when I was (.)
124    there(.) >at this time when I was very calm
125    and relaxed< y'know I could just see that
126    potential (    ) for more interesting
127    things to happen - y'know - not - plenty of
128    (.) good interesting things to happen -
129    y'know [- if] I'm (    ) =
130 T:         [ Yes]
131 C: = different foods to try y'know. "I might be
132    interested in trying that. I wonder what
133    that's like?" [ (.) and (.) ] yet - y'know Jean =
134 T:              [Yes      yes ]
135 C: = I mean (2.5) when I get (    )the-the
136    potential(.) to go from there (.) is massive
137    (.) is enormous-it's unlimited[I think]
138 T:                              [Yes- yes]
139 C: be[cau]se ...
140 T:   [yes]
```

This sequence constitutes an unpacking of how C's new attitude to shopping is related to his state of mind when he is "very calm and relaxed" (lines 124–125). He compares this with his previous attitude when he was "setting myself up for a fall" (line 121).

He can see how he can enjoy shopping, by being able to notice possibilities around him—"I might be interested in trying that. I wonder what that's like?" (lines 131–133). He extrapolates this realisation to a wider view of his life—"the potential to go from there (.) is massive (.) is enormous—it's unlimited I think" (lines 135–137).

Looking at the whole of this sequence (see Appendix 2:3), we can see the way that the kind of devices we have discussed in this chapter work together and influence the procedural consequentiality of the dialogue:

Lines 1–5: T self-discloses followed by question requesting feedback.

Lines 6–57: C elaborates on how he has benefited from T's disclosure leading up to a troubles-telling that constitutes a self-analysis of a new decision he has made.

Lines 58–67: T makes a formulation/candidate elaboration of the changes that C is making in his life and C partially confirms it.

Lines 68–78: T's intervenes, offering information about "how-the-world-is".

Lines 79–100: T intervenes with a formulation/candidate elaboration that is the preface for the beginning of a collaborative elaboration sequence that constitutes the unpacking of C's understanding of T's interpretation.

Lines 103–175: C makes an extensive elaboration that constitutes a story-telling incorporating self analysis.

(16) [JP/Ed2b] Extract from Appendix 2:2

```
39 T: You need an unusual woman. You need a lone-wolf-
40    type woman for your lone-wolf-type man.
      ((laughing tone))
41    (.)
42 C: I'm beginning to realise this and (.) and
43    that also frightens me because - because I was
44    so dependent before
45    (.)
46 T: Yes
47 C: and I think [that] er - my old(.)idea of a =
48 T:           [ yes]
49 C: = relationship w - [was]a very clingy one =
50 T:                    [yes]
51 C: = (.) [ and now] I'm frightened that I'm(.) =
52 T:       [Yes yes]
53 C: = that my new idea (.) if one was not clingy
54    and it sort of frightens me because I keep sort
```

```
55      of thinking "I want to be a little boy again!
56      No! No!" I ha[haha
57 T:              [Haha[hahaha
58 C:                   [Hahahaha "I don't want to
59      grow up!" a clingy one again y'know (.)=
60 T: Exactly. Yes. Exactly. Yes.=
```

The jokey style of T's opening lines 39–40 invites C to respond in a like vein. This seems to intimate that whilst C may make light of his problem, T may not. C accepts the gist of T's prescription (lines 42–44), of "a lone-wolf-type woman for your lone-wolf-type man", but he does not accept the humorous gloss. This is a serious matter. The entire stretch of his elaboration is about his fear of doing again what he has done in the past. This is self-therapy inasmuch it is a retrospective reassessment of his position and his fear that the old pattern of behaviour might recur. T's recipiency is limited to **continuers**, encouragers and affiliative laughter.

(17) Later in the same transcript:
```
126 C: and I feel as if I've gone through the
127    heart of it now and =
128 T: = Yes =
129 C: = I've had relationships and I've stopped
130    drinking and then y'know realised why
131    adolescent relationships [seem] to sort of fit=
132 T:                          [Yes]
133 C: = in very well [with] (.) my recovery [y'know] =
134 T:                [ yes]                  [yes ]
135 C: = and now I can actually feel as if I'm
136    sort of again delaying (.) again delaying (.)
137    until I have time for a relationship (.)
138    [y'know t]ill I have (.) .hhh um it seems to =
139 T: [ Right ]
140 C: = be bothering me less and less (.) y'know
141    and um =
142 T: = ° That's very good. Right.° =
143 C: = and I like to go out with people but it's (.)
144    it's quite confusing at the moment
145    because of the job I'm in. I mean I haven't got
146    the freedom (.) to look for a relationship and
147    yet although it's the wrong time for a
148    relationship (.)I(.) I still (.) want to look
149    for one (.) y'know.
150 T: Yes
151 C: Still the other side of me that's frightened
152    - that's frightened of success (.) I'm almost
```

```
153       frightened of finding somebody y'know (.)
154       Haha[ha
155  T:        [Hahahahaha. Yes.
156  C:   I can see it intellectually. I can see that it
157       would work out much better (.) .hhh if it was
158       done sort of slowly
159  T:   Yes yes.=
160  C:   = because to me the fear of intimac (.) intimacy
161       when I first mentioned before to you (.) I think
162       it was when I first (.) (    ) - it was because
163       someone was coming on very fast towards me and
164       frightened me =
165  T:   = Yes =
```

In lines 126–140, C recognises the progress he has made and takes stock of his present situation. He elaborates on his dilemma, accounting for why it is the wrong time for him to start a relationship, yet he still wants to look for one (line 148–149). In lines 151–164, the theme of fear again surfaces. He is talking his problem through out loud without any help from T, except for the support of her continuers and encouragers. In the process of his analysis of the problem he makes a self-prescription (lines 156–158).

(18) Later in the same transcript
```
166  C:   =and then I realised that (.) That I can stop
167       this. I - I don't have to have this so fast.
168  T:   No - that's right. Yes.
169  C:   Y'know this is not good for me. It's not
170       working for me.[Like] y'[know
171  T:                  [Yes ]
172  T:   Exactly (.) Yes.
173  C:   I feel as if I need to get myself into the
174       position first(.)of being(.)um sort of (.)
175       strong and rested (.)in a way(.)Strong inasmuch
176       as my finances are sort of (.) behind me
177       rather than against me (.) and rested
178       (.)
179  T:   Yes
```

The sort of client talk we see here is very different from the troubles-telling that happens earlier in the work of therapy. Both the above examples reveal characteristics that distinguish the talk as self-therapy. First, there is an acceptance of self-responsibility in lines 173–174, "I need to get myself into the position". Second, the client is beginning to make connections between past and present circumstances.

Third, there is the recognition of progress being made and fourth, although the material is sensitive, the elaborations make sense and are delivered in a relatively unemotional manner.

The application to other domains

The particular conversational devices that I have analysed in this chapter require the highest degree of sensitivity and listening skills. Intense concentration on clients' utterances combined with therapists' ongoing attention to the maintenance of alignment and affiliation is essential for the production of well-timed and relevant interventions. Timing depends on therapists' ability to judge the point when clients are ready to make a more active contribution to the dialogue.

In everyday conversation the kind of strategies I have described would not be appropriate except perhaps in a modified form. For one thing, listening in ordinary conversation is usually sporadic. If we listened to everyone with the degree of concentration shown in the extracts we should soon become very tired.[6] The kind of people who can talk at length are usually those who pay little attention to those they are addressing. They are more intent in having an audience.[7] Noticing how others are responding is either a secondary consideration or is not considered at all. A great deal of everyday conversation comprises phatic talk, showing friendliness and recognising the existence of others. This is a valuable aspect of talk-in-interaction.

Such devices as formulations, candidate elaborations and how they lead to **client elaborations** and **joint production** of the therapeutic process could be very useful in any domain where people are working together to solve a problem of any kind, for their mutual benefit. They could also be adapted to the teaching process in a one-to-one situation where students needs help in becoming aware of their particular difficulties in learning. Much work remains to be done in the exploration of how the way we use language in communication affects our thinking and hampers our lives.

Conclusion

I hope to have brought into focus in this chapter the importance of cooperation between the participants for the unpacking of clients' underlying problems. Emotional affiliation is an essential component and appears in several forms; in the way that therapists pay attention to clients' utterances and give appropriate and varied responses that display careful listening; in therapists joining in with clients' laughter as a way of taking the problem seriously and yet at the same time treating it lightly, which alleviates the painfulness of sensitive issues; in therapists being responsive to clients, i.e., knowing when to talk and when to listen.

I have discussed the various ways in which therapists display their **orientation** to the task of therapy in the skills they use to facilitate the emergence of the underlying problem. Although therapists are in charge of the task, they can develop ways of helping clients to take an active part in the process and eventually learn some of the arts of self-therapy. They can offer models from their own lives and experiences, combining them with professional expertise to give clients the sense that they are not alone in their suffering, and to offer them new points of view which could help them to change unhelpful beliefs and attitudes.

Therapists can offer candidate elaborations to help clients to investigate their feelings and thoughts in greater depth. Clients display that they have absorbed some of the components of the therapeutic task when they begin to recognise the connections between their own past and present events and behaviour in the process of retrospective assessments.

Clients can be seen to take an active part when they produce elaborative sequences spontaneously in order to come to their own conclusions. When psychotherapy is successful, clients grow in confidence in the course of therapy so that they can work on an equal footing with therapists in the unpacking of problems.

In the following chapter I shall examine the findings I have made in this research and consider some of their implications not only for the understanding of the nature of therapy talk but also how this understanding can be disseminated and applied to a wider field.

NOTES

1. There is an ongoing acceptance of the idea that clients can learn to "be their own therapists" (Bohart and Tallman, 1996). This is part of the humanist tradition based on the work of Rogers (1957) and Maslow (1954, 1962). It is based on a tacit assumption that psychotherapy is

not about 'curing' clients' ills or solving their problems; rather it is about facilitating clients to become aware of their own motives and patterns of behaviour so that they can find their own solutions for themselves.

This method applies equally well in education. The etymology of the word education derives from the Latin, *educare*, the leading out of that which lies within, not the imposition by teachers of what they think is knowledge on pupils. This implies respect for the clients or pupils and is a powerful component in the establishment of emotional affiliation and trust, without which useful work cannot be done in either discipline. One of the possibilities of this research is that it may offer tools for classroom relationships.

2. Since upshots "presuppose some unexplicated version of gist" there is always a risk that the co-partipant, in this case the client, may see some hidden agenda on the part of the therapist. In this case, there is a danger that the client might feel the therapist is trying to blame her for not wanting to work with the child. Any suggestion of blame in psychotherapy goes against one of the practice's major tenets—that therapists should be non-judgemental.

3. A common complaint of clients is that they do not feel they are making any progress. A simple way of dealing with this is to remind them of how they were when they first came for therapy (one of the useful aspects of note-taking), as a benchmark against which they can measure how they are now. A characteristic of many of us is that change happens gradually and we often fail to recognise the progress that we are making.

4. Whether or not therapists should make disclosures to clients about their personal lives is a matter of debate. However, as Sacks himself realised, how can people listen properly if they are not allowed to be reminded of their own experiences? I have endeavoured, in the examples I have given, to show that clients appreciate therapists' information about their own experiences. However, this is only the case when that information is warranted by the needs of clients. For instance, if that information provides a model which enables clients to make connections with their own experiences, or if therapists describe some of their own difficulties with life's problems that relate directly, in a helpful way, to clients' acceptance and recognition of their own.

5. The Greek word 'Eureka' as an exclamation of surprise, is attributed to Archimedes, who, having been presented with a gold crown, had doubts about the purity of the metal. He was puzzled about how he could find out if this were the case. Whilst in his bath, musing on the

problem, it occurred to him that water overflowed if an object was put into a full vessel. He suddenly realised that if he took a piece of gold equal in weight to the crown, and immersed both objects in turn into a vessel full of water, he could measure the overflow. If the amount of overflow were not the same, he would then know that the crown was not made of pure gold. In his excitement he dashed out of the house and ran through the streets naked yelling 'Eureka!' which means "I have found it!".

6. Very few clients recognise that psychotherapy is not only tiring for themselves but also for their therapists. It is very easy for all of us to drift off while someone is talking to us. We need a rest from each other more often than we realise. One hundred per cent concentration is not possible. However psychotherapy requires a considerably greater degree of concentration than we usually employ in our everyday interactions.

7. Much more attention is rightly paid today to the importance of good presentation. A major element is the attention of the speaker to the audience. I notice that the best professional seminars I attend are those where lecturers are at pains to involve their audience by breaking up stretches of talk with exercises that illustrate what they are teaching in which the audience participates.

CHAPTER EIGHT

Conclusions

Ongoing attention to relevance, cooperation and coherence and how they are achieved and maintained as key factors in conversation has been a vital aspect of CA research. They cannot be established without the use of both emotional and cognitive skills. My argument is that relevance requires predominantly cognitive skills, cooperation requires predominantly emotional skills and coherence requires both. Attention to relevance makes for the best use of time in psychotherapy. Yet, because it is a cognitive process it does not take into account the consideration of clients' emotions. Thus there is a danger, if the devotion to relevance is too great on the part of the therapist, that it will get in the way of cooperation. Cooperation is not possible in psychotherapy without the establishment of emotional affiliation, which encourages clients to make an active contribution.

Attention to these three requirements prevents conversation from getting into difficulties. Many of the troubles clients bring to therapy have to do with people failing to understand each other, no matter how much they talk. Confusion arises because of the common belief that agreement and good communication are the same thing.

143

It is not realised that agreement is not the same as working towards agreement and agreeing to differ when necessary. Sacks (1992) understood this. He talks about "the magical idea" that "If only we could agree then everything would be alright... There's tremendous hopes involved in what language can do, which are partially involved in overcoming what language does." (Sacks, 1992, p. 433)

Sacks' insight helped me to understand that one of the things I have been trying to do is to discover ways in which we can make better use of language in order to overcome some of the difficulties we create for ourselves through the way we use it. One of the advantages of therapy talk is that the necessity for clients to be as open as possible about their innermost feelings requires new ways in which some of these difficulties can be overcome. The principles of CA derive from how people make sense of each other's utterances. Two key factors are the unpacking of meaning and the recognition that all communication carries some kind of gloss. Hence the understanding of how therapy talk works has multiple implications for the improvement of communication.

Effective communication is dependent on the best use of both cognitive and emotional skills. We have brains to think with, and emotions to feel with. Unless they work together we cannot communicate. The work on **state-related learning** (Rose, 1985) recognises that we learn more easily and effectively when we are relaxed and emotionally comfortable. For this reason it is not surprising that much research into how psychotherapy works has revealed that it is the relationship between the participants that matters, not the particular theoretical approach of the therapist.

In all disciplines that address the solution of problems, relevance is of prime importance. However, when we are working in the dark, a wide exploration of possibilities is necessary because of the problem of not knowing where to start. The same applies to psychotherapy. However, because time is limited, it is essential that, as far as possible, unproductive sequences of talk should be avoided. This poses a major question. How do we know what is important or not? What forms of economy can be applied to the therapeutic dialogue so that the work can be completed in a reasonable length of time?[1] It is this difficulty that gives priority to the question of how relevance is maintained, as far as that is possible, in the practice of psychotherapy.

In this chapter I shall pull together the findings that have come to light as a result of the analysis of the three main features I have identified.

Question and answer

In ordinary conversation the role of questions is similar to their role in psychotherapy: to gather information. However, in psychotherapy, questions are task-driven, therefore their relevance is accepted by clients. For instance, in ordinary conversation, asking a string of questions can cause problems. People can begin to associate such an event with 'cross-questioning' and may challenge the question with another, such as "Why do you want to know?", or, "What are you getting at?", indicating that the questioner may have a covert purpose. The implication here is that where interviewees are clear about the purpose of the **interview**, and feel that it benefits them, task-related constraints are more likely to be accepted.

In ordinary conversation, the tacit social rule is that it is impolite to ask too many questions since they may be seen as unwelcome intrusions into peoples' private lives. The opposite is true in psychotherapy. Its very purpose is to investigate them. Yet, in my data, questions are scarce. Much of the information is gathered in other, less obvious, ways. I would argue that, whilst indirect information surfaces all the time, conscious cooperation only happens when clients feel free enough to talk openly in an environment of trust. It is the responsibility of therapists to create and maintain this setting. The key factor is the affiliation and alignment of the participants.

The particular constraints imposed by questions can be useful in maintaining relevance. For example, when the participants are engaged in collaborative elaboration, questions can be the vehicles for candidate elaborations (see Chapter Six example (10d) and Chapter Seven example (8)). There is a dichotomy here. Why should the question form be used for this purpose?

A candidate elaboration is an interpretation, based on what the therapist already knows about the client. Since it is warranted, it is likely to be confirmed. So why should it be presented in question form that imposes particularly strong constraints to answer affirmatively? It seems that the question form may be doing the work of pointing out and marking the elaboration as being worthy of attention. This interpretation is validated by the fact that in ordinary conversation, questions are pervasively used as vehicles for invitations. A strong invitation, one embedded in a question, could be seen as an affiliative device giving the recipient the message that they are worth inviting.

In Chapter Five we made another surprising discovery. There are far more closed than open questions. In the data, open questions are often problematic for clients. Sometimes they result in relevant information, but more often they need to be followed by closed, i.e., more specific, questions whose greater constraints seem to help clients to talk by offering them a choice of topic. A possible reason for this could be that clients do not know how to start. They hope therapists will have answers they have not been able to discover for themselves. The research Chapters five, six and seven show many occasions when clients expand freely on a topic suggested by the therapist in a closed question.

Looking at questions in terms of what they are doing when they are not actually asking for information, widens the potential for therapists to employ them in different ways in order to use the constraints they impose for benevolent purposes that have to do with affiliation. There is enough evidence in the CA doctor/patient literature that patients have their own ways of avoiding questions they do not wish to answer. Because there are strong constraints to answer does not mean that questioners will get the answer they want.

Troubles-telling

The raw material out of which relevance has to be teased is initially contained in clients' troubles-tellings. Until clients begin to talk, therapists have nothing to go on. Hence the importance of the incitement to talk (Arney & Bergen, 1984). Once this initial target has been achieved, we have seen the evidence in the data that therapists listen carefully for those lexical items and **paralinguistic phenomena** that comprise clues for underlying patterns of belief and behaviour. Troubles-telling is a collaborative achievement. The responses therapists make need to be carefully tailored so that clients feel they are responding in a facilitative way: not merely using conventional continuers like 'uh huh'.

Since in ordinary conversation, members can talk endlessly about their problems, they could assume that they can do the same in psychotherapy.[2] Therefore, one of the skills of therapists is knowing when to interrupt. In the data this happens pervasively when the therapist has got enough information to make a **therapeutic intervention**. Therapists take the initiative in deciding what is or is not relevant in the troubles-telling sequence by virtue of their professional knowledge. By the same token, therapists have the responsibility for creating a comfortable environment that makes it easier for clients to cooperate. This is managed by the use of any one of a number of devices, including questions, candidate elaborations and formulations.

Whatever the intervention its purpose is to draw clients' attention to some feature of the troubles-telling that sheds light on their problem. This could be disjunctive for the troubles-telling, but helpful for relevance and the task of therapy. Therefore such interventions need to be carefully managed by the therapist to maintain both alignment and affiliation with the client.

Another matter that requires attention to relevance is the choice of topic. In psychotherapy there is one simplifying factor. All troubles-talk has an underlying connection with the client's problem. However, sometimes therapists can get caught up in the pursuit of a topic that has no immediate relevance for the problem. In Chapter Six, example (10b), the therapist intervenes to suggest a new sub-topic in her search to find why Christmas was disappointing for Minna; that Christmas was a lot of work for her. The therapist then opens up a chain of question/answer (lines 93–119) which proves to be a blind alley. When this does not work she opens up a second sub-topic in lines 120–122. This proves to be more useful since it leads to the client making an elaboration that suggests a new factor that might be related to her disappointment.

The identification of the client's problem

Cooperation is another of those global categories that means different things in different contexts. Such contexts span a continuum from unwilling cooperation through coercion to cooperation given freely. The factor that accounts for the differences is the degree to which recipients feel it is in their best interests to cooperate. For instance the kind of **interview** where the responses benefit the interviewer only, such as the interrogation of prisoners-of-war, is very different from psychotherapy, where the task is focused on the benefit of the recipient.

We have seen that the placing of constraints is a necessary part of therapists' role as guiders-of-the-work. Satir (1967) sums up the basis of this difference in roles. She argues the importance of therapists taking control of the work:

> "The patient is afraid. He doesn't dare ask about what he doesn't know ... the therapist is not afraid ... he dares to ask questions, and the way he frames them helps the patient to be less afraid as well ... the therapist doesn't know what he doesn't know, but he knows how to find out and how to check on his knowledge." (Satir, 1967, p. 160–161)

Affiliation and alignment are needed for cooperation, and professional knowledge plus knowing how to find out if one does not know are both essential.[3] The participants' roles are different and complementary.

I see the process of clients learning to 'be their own therapists' as a consequence of the kind of cooperation where both participants make an active contribution. The evidence that clients overcome their initial hesitation about working on equal terms with professionals is illustrated in the research chapters in the progression of changes in the patterns of the talk-in-interaction. Clients develop three different skills that they did not have at the onset of therapy. First, they begin to analyse their own stories in order to abstract from them the patterns of their own behaviour as a preliminary to forming their own judgements about changes they are making, and deliberating on how such changes might affect their future lives. This device is called **clients' elaborations**.

Second, they make use of therapists' candidate elaborations to unpack the meaning of their lexical choices in the troubles-tellings. Third, they cooperate with therapists in collaborative elaboration, where the participants work together to resolve the underlying problem in a chain of alternative elaborations. When this stage is reached, continuers and encouragers are not needed. The participants work together on equal terms and reach a consensus that is the result of joint production, rather than the result of therapists imposing answers on clients. This constitutes a new kind of speech-exchange system that has some features in common with troubles-telling, but is of a different order.

Therapists' interventions

Therapists' interventions play an important part in this third feature, the unpacking of the client's underlying problem: the diagnosis of the root of the trouble. The work that they do is both affiliative and relevant. It exhibits both emotional and cognitive features. Interpretations can occur in such positions as during a troubles-telling, during or at the end of a client's account of changed behaviour or changed perceptions, or in other situations. Their most pervasive form constitutes the therapist's identification of a link between past and present behaviour or between past and present attitudes or perceptions. The work they do is to bring to clients' attention that they are indeed making progress through the cognitive recognition that a change has occurred within a framework that provides both emotionally affiliative and cognitively aligned feedback.

When therapists talk about their own difficulties in a neutral manner clients are encouraged to discuss what they perceive as weaknesses in themselves. Such self-disclosures reveal, by their choice of topic, that the selection of a particular difficulty is not arbitrary but is based on clues provided by clients in previous talk. It is warranted. It may constitute an immediately prior turn, or it may be relevant to a client's recurrent theme that runs throughout the sessions. We have also noted that by giving information about their own lives therapists can provide a benchmark against which clients can measure and make sense of their own experience.

Information-giving can be either of the kind that describes an aspect of professional knowledge, or therapists' self-disclosures which may help clients to feel less isolated because they recognise they are not alone. Interventions serve the overall purpose of providing the kind of talk that will jolt clients' memories and incite them to bring relevant information to the surface, a factor that Sacks brought to our notice (1992).

Interpretations can take the form of candidate elaborations. These occur when therapists are trying to help clients to unpack the meaning of a statement or conclusion they have reached. Members are used to getting away with generalisations in ordinary conversation, without having to explain what they mean. However, the special nature of psychotherapy as a problem-solving activity, requires that ambiguities and generalisations be taken apart and specified more precisely.

Clients' responses to therapists' candidate elaborations can be acceptance or rejection, or they can be **clients' elaborations** of therapists' candidate elaborations. A chain of elaborations can be set in motion, where each participant contributes to the unpacking of the problem, as we saw in Chapter Seven. The term for this is **collaborative elaboration**. When the client has absorbed enough knowledge of how therapy is conducted through the talk-in-interaction a new kind of cooperation becomes possible. Both participants work together on equal terms as colleagues to unravel and define the problem.

Therapists do not have to incite this kind of talk from clients. It arises spontaneously during sessions only after the preliminary work of troubles-telling with therapists' feed-back and more troubles-telling with interventions including interpretations has been done. By that time clients are beginning to be more aware of what is going on. They are clearer about what is troubling them, and they are beginning to make greater use of therapists' devices. Clients may still tell stories with a beginning, a middle and an end, but they are related to the new understandings they are making through their increasing ability to analyse their own behaviour.

This occurs when clients begin to be aware of what they need to change in their life, or when they have the Eureka! experience. Either way, such accounts are, like all talk, procedurally consequential to what has gone before. Therefore it is not surprising that a major feature of clients' self-therapy involves a change in clients' mind-set, a new point of view.

One of the ways of maintaining coherence in ordinary conversation is by the use of formulaic utterances. Proverbs are the most common example of this feature. Because of the need for mutual understanding we do not have the time to find out what every word that another person uses means. Therefore ordinary talk is full of short cuts that work for a necessary economy. A conversation can be deemed to be coherent when both interlocutors feel that they know what they are talking about. However this can be an illusion. They may be using the same words in quite different ways. In reality, the reason many people feel they are 'not communicating' is because of this economy.

Sacks (1992) was aware of the difficulties that arise in language use. One of the problems is that we think we understand what others are saying when we only partly understand. This surface understanding is reinforced by the use of formulaic utterances of all kinds.

The problem is caused by the belief that such utterances are common sense wisdom and therefore unchallengeable. In Chapter Six, example (10), we have discussed "people are all the same" as a formulaic utterance worthy of investigation because we do not know precisely what it means, yet it is used by the client more than once as representing some kind of truth. Once the meaning has been unpacked (see Appendix 2:1) we can see that the underlying disappointment has to do with the client's belief that people failed to give the client the supportive response she needed after a serious illness. Here is an explanation that we can all understand, whereas "people are all the same" is an enigmatic statement, which could mean different things to different people in different contexts. One of the most satisfying of my discoveries about therapy talk is that they shed light on what we are doing in everyday talk.

Similarities and differences between everyday talk and therapy talk.

Similarities

- They entail fewer constraints than other speech-exchange systems.
- They entail fewer direct questions than other speech-exchange systems.
- Ordinary conversation has more in common with psychotherapy talk than with most other institutional sites.
- Emotional affiliation, as well as alignment, is important for them both.
- The telling of first and second stories plays a part in each domain.

Differences

- The purpose of the talk is different. In psychotherapy one participant seeks professional help from the other.
- Clients are encouraged to talk. They do not have to stake a claim to embark on a troubles-telling. The purpose of troubles-telling in therapy is to provide information. In ordinary conversation it can be a bid for affiliation.
- Therapists make interventions that are task-related. They can interrupt when they choose. Interruptions in ordinary conversation can be problematic.

- Generalisations and formulaic utterances are challenged in psycho-therapy, and clients are encouraged to unpack them. In everyday conversation they are accepted. Their meaning is not questioned.
- In psychotherapy the selection of topic is not arbitrary. It is intended to be relevant to the task. If a topic turns out to be irrelevant it is discarded.
- Therapists' troubles-telling and self-disclosure serve a different purpose in psychotherapy. They are devices for helping clients to remember their own experiences.
- Like other institutional domains, psychotherapy is time limited as well as task-oriented. These constraints result in a more structured form than in mundane conversation.
- The need to listen carefully is greater than in ordinary conversation. Because of the elusive nature of the problem, attentive listening can be more important than in other institutional domains.
- The sensitive nature of the client's problem increases the need for, first, the aptness and positioning of such features as encouragers, and second, the skilful use of affiliation and alignment by the therapist.
- In psychotherapy the emphasis is on the structure of a problem, not the content. In everyday conversation, Sacks (1992) argues that members avoid 'abstract conversation'. Yet in psychotherapy, the whole thrust of the task is towards abstraction of the elements of the problem. This is revealed in the recurrent establishment of connections between past and present events by both participants. It is not detailed descriptions of the events themselves that are important, but their shared structure.

This outline of similarities and differences between psychotherapy and other speech-exchange systems highlights the special nature of psychotherapy. As a result of these findings it is now possible to see how they could be used as a basis for further research and for practical use.

Conclusion

The body of research that began with Harvey Sacks' seminal work forty years ago was slow to get started. It was ahead of its time, and, like many revolutionary ideas, posed a threat to some aspects of accepted knowledge. Over the last fifteen years the use of **conversation analysis** methodology has increased at an exponential rate.

Nevertheless, I believe that we are only just scratching the surface of its possibilities.

In the field of psychotherapy, there remains much research work to be done. Looking back on my PhD study, I realise that I have prepared a foundation for further studies. By outlining some of the main features of psychotherapy, as revealed by my data, and attempting to give some idea of when and how they are used within extended and complete-in-themselves stretches of therapy talk, I hope to have provided a framework within which more understanding of the overall organisation of this practice can become possible.

Following the ideas of Thomas Kuhn (1962), I see **conversation analysis** as a paradigm, a framework that, by imposing constraints of a particular type, makes it possible for certain conclusions to be reached. Nevertheless, since change is necessary, and indeed cannot be held back, we inevitably come across anomalies within the framework. Without such a paradigm we should not notice the anomalies. By limiting ourselves, we make it possible not only to conduct research in a disciplined manner but also to draw attention to those findings that do not fit the paradigm. Such findings constitute the beginning of a new paradigm.

Paradigms themselves, like everything else, including how we use language, are subject to change. The paradox is that effective change can take place only within a recognised framework, without which new ideas would have no basis for growth. Part of the value of having a number of set beliefs is that as society changes, some of them stand out as redundant precisely because they become noticeable through their increasingly inhibitive effect on changing situations and people's reactions to them. Hence, what is often seen as rigidity is necessary and has its purpose.[4]

I have outlined how constraints work in psychotherapy: how they can be used effectively to keep the work of therapy on track. Such work is only possible when there is goodwill on both sides. Cooperation becomes possible when clients feel they have freedom to say what they want, yet at the same time understand that some constraints are necessary if the task of therapy is to be accomplished. In the final stages of both short and more extended boundaried stretches of talk, I hope to have shown that these constraints tend to lessen as clients begin to learn the skills of self-therapy and demonstrate this in their management of collaborative elaboration as a tool for both diagnosis and treatment.

The very fact that it is possible in psychotherapy to develop a particular type of activity and speech exchange system, building on what the participants recognise as ordinary conversation, has vast implications not only for human communication but also for the understanding of how the mind works. The possibilities, both for the understanding of the process of psychotherapy and how people create meaning for themselves and each other seem to me to be limitless.

NOTES

1. Freudian psychoanalysis and Jungian analytical psychology were both designed to explore patients' lives in depth, which is why both methods can require attendance at sessions of up to five times a week and can go on for years. Such a leisurely and expensive process does not sit well with our busy age. The concept of 'brief therapy' has come into being because many people need urgent help, and need it quickly. Therefore there are useful new approaches that focus on addressing specific problems and providing quick changes. However, the stronger the underlying conflict that needs to be resolved, the longer it takes for changes to occur, although there are some remarkable people who seem to be able to speed up the process. Attention to focus and relevance in psychotherapy can minimise the length of time needed for effective work.
2. A constant dilemma for therapists is maintaining the focus on relevance to the problem. Some clients would talk forever and get nowhere if permitted to do so. Knowing when and when not to intervene and how to intervene requires highly developed skills that have only been touched on in the research. Such skills would also be very useful in ordinary conversation. A big problem for members is knowing when and how to open up openings as well as closings.
3. Too much importance can be attributed to affiliation. Professional knowledge matters. Without it therapists would not have a basis to work from to help them to recognise how certain types of human behaviour are manifested through talk: transference and counter transference for example, a vital Freudian concept the value of which is accepted by the overwhelming majority of therapists, though they may call it by a different name.
4. Pirsig's two novels (1974 & 1991) constitute an interesting exposition of the conflict between conformity and change that is both erudite and highly readable.

Glossary

A3N (account apparently appropriate, negativer) This device serves as a justification for an opinion, e.g., "everybody thinks so" (Sacks, 1992, p. 23).

adjacency pair This is the smallest unit of conversation, e.g., one person asks a question of another who then replies.

affiliation The efforts of a listener to respond in a way which gives emotional support to clients.

affiliative responses These can take the form of **continuers, change-of-state tokens** and **paralinguistic responses**.

alignment A cognitive activity where listeners' responses serve to maintain **relevance** by making sure they are talking about the same thing (see **topic**).

ambivalence The meaning of words depends on the **context** of the subject under discussion and on the person using them.

appositionals Words such as 'well' 'but' and 'so'. "They are turn-entry devices, or pre-starts, in contrast with tag-questions, which are exit-devices or post-completers." (Sacks, Schegloff & Jefferson, 1974, p. 719). They can be **markers** for the beginning of an **utterance**. Hutchby (1999) calls them buffer devices because they seem to mark the places where one activity-type ends and another begins. Perhaps the purpose of this usage is to give speakers a moment to adapt to the change.

candidate elaboration A therapist's offering of an interpretation of the client's meaning, when the client is having difficulty in explaining clearly, containing a suggestion which the client can refuse, partially accept or accept.

categorisations Sacks uses the term characterisation. Edwards (in Antaki & Widdicombe (1998) differentiates between two basic types of categorisation: the cognitive/psychological stance of Rosch et alia (1976) & Lakoff (1987), where the focus is on how the mind works and Sacks' view that social activities are conducted through conversation between participants who categorise themselves and each other (and whose categorisation of self and others is continuously changing. See **membership categorisation device (MCD)**).

change-of-state tokens A **marker**, an exclamation displaying a therapist's emotional change (i.e., surprise) at receiving new information. Atkinson & Heritage (1984) demonstrate how, in dictionaries, 'Oh' and laughter are carriers for the expression of "emotions, amusements, approval and the like". (Atkinson & Heritage, 1984, p. 297)

clients' elaborations Clients' analyses of their own stories when they assess changes they are making as a preliminary for understanding what the impact might be on their future.

closed question One referring to a specific topic where there is a strong constraint to answer: i.e., "How old are you?".

coherence The process whereby participants make sense of each other's **utterances** in order to clear up misunderstandings on-the-spot. Coherence requires **cooperation** and **relevance**.

collaborative elaboration **Cooperation** between therapist and client in resolving the underlying problem in a **chain** of alternative **elaborations**.

context Defines the meaning of **lexical items** used in a particular kind of activity.

continuers Token responses that confirm to the speaker that the recipient is listening, e.g., 'yes' and 'uh huh' (Schegloff, 1982). They can also be used as **markers** and exit-devices, reinforcing clients' insights and allowing a move on to new **topics**.

Conversation Analysis (CA) The study of "naturally-occurring talk-in-interaction" through the analysis of the actual **utterances** spoken by the participants (Hutchby & Wooffitt, 1998, p. 6).

cooperation A process of participants working together to achieve the resolution of a problem. Cooperation is defined by Pain (2003) in a particular way in the process of psychotherapy. Therapists and clients play complementary roles. Clients alone have full access to themselves; therapists have theoretical knowledge of psychological processes from their training, and practical knowledge from their own experiences. For successful work both parties need to make a contribution with the aim

at arriving at a consensus on the nature of the problem and the prognosis of possible solutions for the problem.

decision Clients' decisions whether to accept, partially accept or
reject therapists' **elaborations/formulations.**

elaboration A process of unpacking meaning that can be done by
both therapists and clients.

ethnomethodology A branch of anthropology initiated by Garfinkel
on the importance of the study of everyday human behaviour and how
it varies in different cultures. Goffman's work attended to such matters
as rituals and human role-playing in social interactions.

Eureka! factor A strongly emotional and immediate recognition of a
discovery.

extreme case formulation A disclaimer, e.g., 'it's never like that'
which, in everyday conversation, is rarely challenged because it presupposes that no further explanation is necessary. This device was recognised by Pomerantz (1986).

footing The role a person plays at any time (Goffman, 1979). Hutchby
(1999) shows that the roles people play in conversation are constantly
changing as sequences of conversation fulfil different tasks.

formulaic language Related to **extreme case formulations, A3N** and
proverbs, where a statement of a traditionally accepted opinion is tacitly
accepted as a fact. The purpose of the device is to appeal to recipients
to accept a generally held opinion as a fact, thereby preventing them
from challenging the veracity of the statement. **Formulaic language** is
beloved by tyrants and all forms of totalitarian governments as an effective weapon to prevent people thinking for themselves.

formulation Paraphrasing by therapists to enable clients to unpack
the meaning of what they are trying to communicate.

generalisations Lexical terms or phrases that stand for a whole range
of meanings. Edwards & Potter (1992) discuss two main factors in the
analysis of description—**rhetoric** and the reconstruction of past events.
See **gloss**.

gloss Everything is said for a purpose (Garfinkel & Sacks, 1970). The
way in which an **utterance** is made is a vehicle for the purpose of the
speaker. This may be overt or covert. Mark Anthony's speech "Friends,
Romans, countrymen, lend me your ears" in Shakespeare's play 'Julius
Caesar', whilst ostensibly backing up Caesar's assassinators, was cov-
ertly condemning them, an excellent example of how someone with
exceptional skills of eloquence and **rhetoric** can manipulate others.

habit A behaviour pattern that becomes automatic once it has become
established in the brain as a new neural pathway.

idealised cognitive model (ICM) A term created by Lakoff (1987),
who subscribes to the irrefutable belief that the world is too complex to be
entirely understood, and therefore we need a series of models, all of which

are approximations, to guide us in our actions and thoughts. For example, the way we categorise time into hours, days, weeks etc. does not exist in nature, but without it we would be at a loss to manage time. See **categorisations, generalisations,** and **membership categorisation device.**

indexical related to the use of words.

intersubjectivity Atkinson & Heritage (1984) describe the term intersubjectivity as a number of devices whereby participants in conversation understand each other. Interactive understanding depends on several factors ... how both participants orient themselves to what they are trying to achieve ... how they make sense of prior turns ... a mutual consensus about how they see the world in general ... how they adjust to ongoing changes of context." (Pain, 2003).

intervention Any one of a number of devices that involve therapists' intervening to make a relevant comment or suggestion on what is going on both in the talk and in the search for a diagnosis of the problem and its possible resolution.

interview A dialogue where one person seeks information from another for a specific purpose. Interviews can take three forms: first, structured, e.g., courtroom proceedings; second, semi-structured, e.g., psychotherapy and third, unstructured, where the interviewer's main role is that of listener (Hutchby & Wooffitt, 1998).

intrasubjectivity The internal dialogue that continuously operates inside us all both when we are talking and when we are alone. It can operate consciously and unconsciously. Without it we would not be able to make sense of what others say to us. This process of intrasubjectivity enables us to check out through our own experiences and belief systems everything we take in and to construct a response.

joint production The result of a therapist and client working together each taking an active part to form a consensus on a diagnosis and prognosis for the future.

lexical item A concrete, specific object in the form of a word. In CA we take the concrete and extract its meaning as best we can. The ambivalence of words often causes unnecessary arguments because of the different ways in which we, as individuals, understand them.

linguistics Sacks (1992) posited that the term 'linguistics' comprises much more than the study of fixed grammatical rules which cover the structure of sentences and the meaning of words. Why should we not change the study of sentences to that of **utterances?** Levinson (1983) describes a sentence as "an abstract theoretical entity defined by a theory of grammar and an utterance as "a sentence, sentence analogue or sentence fragment in an actual context which fulfils the action of a speech act." (Levinson, 1983, p. 18) It can be as little as one word where that one word *does* something. Thus 'utterance' covers a much wider range of meaningful groups of words than 'sentence'. This probably why Sacks considered that "the notion of utterance has been very productive for research." (Sacks, 1992, p. 647)

marker A **lexical item** that adds emphasis, e.g., 'You did that all on your own? REALLY?'

member Person belonging to a particular social group, which could be of any type or size, e.g., all those over seven feet tall, all those who have children, all those who have had over fifty paid jobs.

membership categorisation device (MCD) Members' on-the-spot ability to categorise themselves and others (Sacks, 1992).

metaconstructions Umbrella words (Siegfried, 1995) that can cover a number of meanings, see **generalisations**.

narrative therapy The result of therapists' encouragement of clients to come to terms with past experiences by reconstructing them (McLeod, 2000). See **retrospective reassessments**.

open question A question where the response is subject to minimum constraints, e.g., 'How are you?' which leaves recipients free to respond in any way they like. Pain's (2003) findings show that open questions tend to appear at the beginning of sessions and **closed questions** during clients' **troubles-telling**, where clarification is needed.

orientation The role of the person speaking. One person plays the role of therapist, the other, the role of client in psychotherapy. See **categorisation** and **frame attunement**.

paralinguistic phenomena Non-verbal communications such as the tone, volume or speed of the voice and silences between **turns**.

paralinguistic responses Non-verbal responses such as tears or laughter.

polyglot category A category which can be broken down into sub-categories.

procedural consequentiality In conversation each **turn** is affected by the previous turn. The procedure is that interlocutors make their own sense of each other's **utterances** and design their own utterances in response to that interpretation.

professional dominance This idea originated in sociological medical research (Heath, 1992). The traditional role of doctor/patient is asymmetrical and leaves little room for the patient's opinions.

proverbs Traditional lexical phrases that are metaphorical formulae for some aspect of truth: e.g., 'a rolling stone gathers no moss' is a statement of folklore wisdom that if you make changes too often, you will learn nothing.

receipt tokens Therapists' brief responses that acknowledge what clients have said.

relevance Adherence to the **topic** and to the task of therapy.

repair A series of devices whereby we correct our own and each other's **turns**.

retrospective reassessment Clients' strategies of re-telling past events with a new **gloss** because of new understandings.

rhetoric The **gloss** we give **utterances** through our lexical choices to convey a certain impression.

self-disclosure Therapists tell details from their own experiences to encourage clients to discuss theirs.

speech-exchange systems "ways in which **turn**-taking can be organised to carry our social tasks ... [involving] **talk-in-interaction**." (Sacks, Schegloff & Jefferson, 1974).

spin See **gloss**.

stake inoculation A preliminary way of discounting the significance of an action, for example "To be honest", or "I'm not being funny, but ...". (Potter, 1997, p. 138)

state-related learning The emotional state we are in when we are learning affects how quickly and effectively we can absorb new information (Rose, 1985).

talk-in-interaction Two or more people talking together to complete a social task.

therapeutic intervention Any one of a number of devices where the therapist intervenes for the purpose of forwarding the task of therapy.

tokens Acknowledgements of previous speaker's **utterances**, usually the province of therapists responding to clients. They are essentially brief: either **lexical items** or phrases.

topic The subject of a conversation, agreed by both participants.

troubles-telling Stories that clients tell to therapists about their life difficulties. In Pain's (2003) data, the structure of these stories changes dramatically to the point where clients move away from an emotional activity towards a cognitive analysis of their problems which includes some kind of diagnosis and prognosis.

turn One person speaks in a conversation.

upshot A therapist's device: a technique for presenting a **candidate elaboration** that contains the presupposition of some unexplicated version of gist/underlying meaning.

utterance "a unit of speech communication from a short single word rejoinder in dialogue to the large novel or scientific treatise" (Bakhtin, 1994, p. 82). "a sentence, sentence analogue, or sentence fragment, in an actual context which fulfils the action of a speech act." (Levinson, 1983, p. 18). An utterance "covers a wider range of meaningful groups of words than a sentence."

warranted Whenever a therapist makes a suggestion or interpretation to a client, it should be warranted: i.e., it should be based on evidence from what the client has already disclosed.

APPENDIX 2

Transcription key

The transcription symbols are common to Conversation Analysis, and were developed by Gail Jefferson (Hutchby & Wooffitt, 1998).

(.)	A pause in the talk-noticeable but too small to be measured.
(0.5)	The number in brackets indicates a pause of 0.5 seconds or more measured in tenths of a second.
=	Indicates that one utterance follows seamlessly from the prior turn.
[ ]	Square brackets between adjacent lines positioned immediately over each other indicate overlapping talk.
.hh	This symbol indicates an intake of breath by the speaker. The more h's the longer the inbreath.
hh	This symbol indicates an outbreath. The more h's the longer the outbreath.
( )	Empty parentheses indicate a spate of talk that is not clear enough to be transcribed.
(( ))	A double bracket indicates a non-verbal activity such as the clearing of a throat or laughter as described by the transcriber.
-	A dash indicates a sharp cutting off of a word.
:	Colons indicate the stretching out of a word. The more colons, the more the word is stretched.

<u>Underlining</u>	Underlining indicates that the speaker is emphasising a particular word.
CAPITALS	Capitals indicate speech louder than the surrounding context of talk.
° °	Degree signs round a spate of talk indicate that it is noticeably quieter than the surrounding talk.
> <	'More than' and 'less than' signs indicate that the talk they encompass is noticeably faster than the surrounding talk. The speeding up of the language can act as a marker for the disjunctiveness of this spate of talk from the surrounding talk.
–>	Arrows point to a specific part of the transcription that is under discussion.

APPENDIX 2:1

Transcriptions

[JP/M1/11101]
```
 1 T: .hh Right Minna. So hhh you - you were
 2    telling me that you were
 3    disappointed about Christ [mas]
 4 C:                          [Yes. I'm
 5    always disappointed.
 6 T: Always?
 7 C: Oh [yes.
 8 T:    [Yes so could you give me a bit more
 9    informa[tion?
10 C:        [I was talking to someone just
11    after Christmas at a party and er (0.8)
12    and we was (.) she was saying that um (.)
13    a lot of people were disappointed about
14    Christmas. And when you think about it -
15    It's just that before Christmas - you know
16    when you see on the telly and get -(.)
17    preparing for Christmas=
18 T: = Yes =
19 C: = and um I just had it in my mind that it
20 T: was going to be (.) the ideal Christ
21    [mas and all the] family's going to be=
```

```
22      [Oh I see]
23 M: = there and we're all y'know sitting around
24      the fire [and] playing games [and] it's=
25 T:           [yes]                [yes]
26 M: = never like [that.
27 T:              [Hahaha I s[ee hahahahaha
28 M:                         [except that (.)
29      I (.) in my mind every year I think it's
30      going to be that w[ay a]nd so all the=
31 T:                     [Yes]
32 M: = people come along. My daughter came home
33      with her boy friend and his mother came
        because
34      she's on her own =
35 T: = Oh I see =
36 M: = and I said "Well bring her down" and my
37      great-uncle was there and lots of people
38      were there but um (.) then it's all over with
39      and it's just not (.) I think (.) well (.)
40      y'know a lot of pressure and spending and
41      at the end of the day people are just the
42      same as ever.
        ((laughing tone))
43 T: Haha[hahaha
44 C:      [And I've got - my great-uncle is
45      ninety-two and he's very gropy with women
46      y'kn[ow= ((laughing tone))
47 T:      [Oh I see hahahahaha
48 C: =this lady ca (.) and any new lady on the
49      scene y'know [he loves it] and then he=
50 T:               [Oh yes I see]
51 C: = puts his hand on her kn[ee (.)] I could=
52 T:                          [ Yes  ]
53 C: = See her squirming and (.) very (.) um
54      tou[chy-feely
55 T:     [Yes yes.
56      Well that's the bit that bother[s you.
57 C:                                  [But
58      it - yeah. He thinks because he's
59      ninety-two he can =
60 T: = get away with it = (( laughing tone))
61 C: = at ninety two. So I defend the wo[men you=
62 T:                                     [Hahaha
63 C: =[know
```

64 T: [Hahaha. Has he done it all his life?
65   (0.6)
66 C: No (.) no becau[se
67 T: [it may be just because
68   he thinks he's licen[sed be]cause he's=
69 C: [Yes]
70 T: ninety t[wo years old.
71 C: [Yes (.) yes.
72 T: Oh right. Yes. So what (.) How would you like
73   Christmas to be?
74 C: ° I don't know °
75 T: Do you get a strong sense of (.) pleasure
76   from having all the family together?=
77 C: = NO! ((both laugh))
78 T: YES! (.) ° I was wondering ° that's what
79   makes it good (.) is to have the people
80   you really want around you?
81 C: No. I think I'd be better off with a bunch
82   of strangers.   [Hahahahaha
83 T: [REALLY? right (.) right. Even
84   your husband and your children?
85 C: Oh (.) with my husband and my daughter - but
86   (.) um =
87 T: But not with those others! Hahahahaha.
88 C: It's because we live in a large house and
89   we've got plenty of room and so everyone
90   assumes whenever there's a holiday um - Oh
91   we'll all go round to Minna's house (   )
92   and everyone arrives a[nd
93 T: [It's a lot of work
94   then?
95 C: It is when they go - the changing the
96   sheets.
97 T: I see (.) right. So how many people were
98   there?
99 C: Um (.) Well there were only seven of us
100   for Christmas lunch and the next day all
101   our children came cos we've got eight
102   children between us and now they've all
103   got partners so that's immediately
104   sixteen [and a]=
105 T: [Oh I see]
106 C: = grandchild and it's all just spread out.
107 T: I see. You've got a very big table, have

108   you?
109 C: YEAH. But my husband loves entertaining.
110 T: Oh DOES he?
111 C: "Oh come round!" he says =
112 T: = And he's the life and soul of the party
113   is he? =
114 C: = Yes (.) yes.
115 T: Oh (.) Right. So who does all the cooking?
116 C: Oh he does. He loves all the cooking and
117   everything. He's brilliant.
118 T: So he thoroughly enjoys himself?
119 C: Yes.
120 T: So what would you rather that you (.) you
121   could have your children and get rid
122   of these others?
123 C: Yes (.) I'm alright for a short space of
124   time - like you say - I'm alright in a (   )
125   and then I've had enough =
126 T: = Yes =
127 C: = but by that time people have all had a
128   bit to drink and they're ready to - heh heh-
129   carry on round [the table
130 T: [Hahaha well what do they
131   do when they carry on round the table? What
132   are they actually talking about? Playing
133   games?
134 C: Yeah. Yeah=
135 T: = and you don't really enjoy it?
136 C: Up to a point.
137 T: ° Yes (.) yes °
138   (3.00)
139 C: I just found it disappointing because (.)
140   I don't know if it was (.) I don't know if
141   it was just this year - I don't know if
142   it was because I'd been ill and I thought
143   this was going to be the ultimate Christmas
144   just - in fact I didn't think I was going
145   to be here this Christmas =
146 T: = Oh I see (   ) Yes (.) yes.
147 C: I wanted it to be this ultimate Christmas =
148 T: = Yes I see so because you thought it was
149   such a wonderful thing [to] to be alive to =
150 C: [Yes]
151 T: be here for Christmas therefore you

```
152     expected it to be sort of something
153     wonderful.
154     (.)
155 C:  Yes.
156 T:  I see - something out of the u[sual.
157 C:                              [Yes I did.
158     People are still the same though.
159 T:  Yes hahaha
160 C:  My illness was never mentioned by anybody
161     [and
162 T:  [Uh huh. Would you rather it was mentioned?
163 C:  I don't know.
164 T:  You mean people ignored the fact that
165     you'd been ill? =
166 C:  = YEAH =
167 T:  = is that what you're getting at?
168 C:  YEAH. And it (.) ° I suppose that (.) they
169     didn't realise that I wanted it to be
170     that special Christmas.°
171 T:  ° What could they have done differently if
172     they'd known that?°
173 C:  Well. They couldn't have done anything
174     as they couldn't have changed. They'd
175     still have been the same people. My old uncle
185     would have still been (.) If he could have had
186     the day off from molesting women =
187 T:  = Ha ha ha =
188 C:  = It would have lessened the anxiety of that cos
189     I apologised to my daughter's future mother-in-law
190     I said "I'm so sorry about it" (.) She said "I've
191     got used to it now. This is the second day. I brace
192     myself now when he comes into the room.
           (laughing tone)
193 T:  Hahaha
194 C:  It's awful Jean
195 T:  Yes (.) Yes quite =
196 C:  = So there again I put it out of my mind.
197     [I see I'd hurt too ] many friends
198 T:  [Yes. I see. Yes ]
199 T:  Yes I see (.) Mm. So in a way it's because
200     Christmas was the same way it's always
201     been =
202 C:  = Mm =
203 T:  = and it was disappointing
```

204   (.)
205 C: Yes.
206 T: I think it's also something to do with
207   you've had a very difficult year.
208 C: Yes.
209 T: And not one person acknowledged =
210 T: = "Minna's had a tough time"
211 C: YES. That would have been LOVELY!
212 T: Yes. It would have been some
213   recognition - I can understand that.
214 C: Can you?
215 T: Yes (.) Yes.

APPENDIX 2:2

[JP/Ed2b/2829]

```
 1 T: This is what I've been interested in since I
 2     was five and I've done masses and masses of
 3     reading. It's like painting. I started to
                ((laughing tone))
 4     paint five years ago. OK I can paint
 5     reasonably well but painting isn't the thing I
 6     do best(.)and so now(.)when I'm doing what I
 7     want to do that I know I do best and er (.)and
 8     it's immensely satisfying and I'm actually
 9     (.) no longer going out and spending much of my
10     money like I used to because I don't want to (.)
11     because of the very satisfaction of (.) of just
12     doing the studying.
13     (.)
14 C: Yes
15 T: so (.) and I think this applies to all of us
16     that we need to find to find out what we really
17     want to do (.) and give ourselves up to it (.)
18     and then (.) then I think (.) it can't help but
19     succeed.
20     (.)
```

21 C: Yes (1.0) yes
22 T: And when it comes to relationships (.) in a way
23   (.) you get your relationship with your work
24   right (.) you also get your relationship with
25   people right as well because there's a
26   connection.
27   (.)
28 C: Er (.) yes (.) yes (.) I realise I feel like
29   that (2.6) I would mix with the right sort of
30   people by doing work I like doing y'know (.)
31   I - I would be myself y'know and um hhh
32   (.)
33 T: So you're going to need a very special kind
34   of woman. You're not going to nee(.) need (.)
35   well you know that - you know you don't - you
36   want a woman who's exciting and who (.) does
37   things and this lady (.) this Czechoslovakian
38   lady sounds like a very unusual woman because
39   you need an unusual woman. You need a lone-wolf-
40   type woman for your lone-wolf-type man.
                     ((laughing tone))
41   (.)
42 C: I'm beginning to realise this and (.) and
43   that also frightens me because - because I was
44   so dependent before
45   (.)
46 T: Yes
47 C: and I think [that] er - my old (.) idea of a =
48 T: [Yes]
49 C: = relationship w (.) [was] a very clingy one =
50 T: [Yes]   ]
51 C: = (.) [and now] I'm frightened that I'm (.)that=
52 T: [Yes yes]
53 C: = my new idea (.)if one was not clingy (.) and
54   it sort of frightens me because I keep sort of
55   thinking "I want to be a little boy again!"
56   No! No! I Haha[ha
57 T: [hahahaha[hahaha
58 C: ["I don't want to grow
59   up!" a clingy one again y'know =
60 T: = Exactly. Yes. Exactly. Yes.=
61 C: =and that sort of does (.) sort of frighten
62   me =
63 T: = Yes. Well it's not either or [because]if you=

```
64 C:                              [It isn't]
65 T: = look at it that way in a way we all want to be
66     a bit clingy sometimes.
67 C: Yes.
68 T: We all need support from our partners right?
69     But there's a difference between being clingy
70     and being supported (.)[It's] not the same =
71 C:                           [Yeah]
72 T. = because no matter how independent you are (.)
73     it's lovely to feel that there is one other
74     person that is there for you (.) to give you
75     support.
76 C: Right.
77 T: But it doesn't have to be a clingy relationship.
78     It's what they call interdependent. Rather
79     than being dependent the key in-word now for
80     relationships is interdepen[dence(.)wh]ere=
81 C:                             [yes ah yes]
82 T: =you are each (.)depend on each other (.) but
83     you can function on your own -and the most
84     important thing is being able to function on
85     your own.
86     (.)
87 C: yes
88 T: and it's far more satisfying because if you
89     have that relationship (.)You're really
90     relating to another (.) grown-up person.
91     You're not relating to somebody (.) who wants
92     to be part of you. You're keeping your
93     separateness and enjoying your separateness
94     together.
95     (.)
96 C: Yeah (.[yes
97 T:         [that's what a good mature relationship
98     is.
99 C: Hh I feel as if (.) intellectually I'm getting
100    to understand the - to understand(.) what a
101    relationship is because when I see it
102    ((clears throat)) (.)
103    and they put so much emphasis on relationships
104    y'know and even (.) even (.) I've got a doctor
105    friend and I've got another one who's (.) um (.)
106    um (.) insolvency um (.) um (.) in insolvency
107    business y'know (    ) a consultant (.) an
```

```
108    insolvency consultant (.) who ran his own =
109 T: = Yeah =
110 C: = business and then he went broke ((clears
111    throat)).And you (.) you know he's got degrees
112    in this and the other's got y'know doctor's
113    degrees y'know and yet they would be sort of
114    like nothing (.) exceptions like women and
115    where's the next relationship coming from y'know
116    and there are relationships that have been
117    absolutely disastrous because of clinging on to
118    women.
119 T: Yes =
120 C: =And yet they're still doing it y'know. And
121    then I realize it's - I can see it in them
122    that it's this growing-up thing that
123    they're going through except that they're the
124    same age as me.
125    (.)
126 C: and I feel as if I've gone through the
127    heart of it now and =
128 T: = Yes =
129 C: = I've had relationships and I've stopped
130    drinking and then y'know realised why
131    adolescent relationships [seem]to sort of fit=
132 T:                          [ Yes]
133 C: = in very well [with] (.) my recovery [y'know]=
134 T:                [Yes ]                   [ Yes ]
135 C: = and now I can actually feel as if I am sort
136    of again delaying (.) again delaying (    )
137    until I have time for a relationship (.)
138    [y'know t]ill I have (.) .hhh um. It seems to=
139 T: [ Right ]
140 C: = be bothering me less and less (.) y'know (.)
141    and um =
142 T: = ° That's very good. Right.° =
143 C: = and I like to go out with people but it's
144    (.) it's quite confusing at the moment
145    because of the job I'm in. I mean I haven't got
146    the freedom (.) to look for a relationship and
147    and yet although it's the wrong time for a
148    relationship I (.) I still (.) want to look
149    for one (.) y'know.
150 T: Yes.
151 C: Still the other side of me that's frightened
```

```
152      - that's frightened of success (.) I'm almost
153      frightened of finding somebody y'know (.)
154      Haha[ha
155 T:       [Hahahahahah. Yes.
156 C: I can see it intellectually. I can see that it
157      would work out much better (.) .hhh if it was
158      done sort of slowly
159 T: Yes yes
160 C: because to me the fear of intimac (.) intimacy
161      -when I first mentioned before to you(.) I think
162      was when I first (.) (    )- it was because
163      someone was coming on very fast towards me and
164      frightened me =
165 T: = yes =
166 C: = and then I realised that (.) that I can stop
167      this. I don't have to have this so fast
168 T: No (.)that's right. Yes.
169 C:  y'know this is not good for me. It's not
170      working for me (.)[Like] y'know.
171 T:                    [Yes ]
172      Exactly (.) Yes.
173 C: I feel as if I need to get myself into the
174      position first (.) of being (.) um sort of (.)
175      strong and rested (.) in a way. Strong inasmuch
176      as my finances are sort of (.) behind me rather
177      than against me (.) and rested
178      (.)
179 T: Yes
180 C: inasmuch as I haven't got the sort of (.)
181      stresses like (.) like I've got at the moment
182      y'kn[ow.] I've just not got enough money =
183 T:     [Yes]
184 C: = really (.) and the car's breaking down. I'm
185      sort of struggling with all the bank payments
186      [and] everything and having quite a workload=
187 T: [Yes]
188 C: = and wanting to do something else (.) I feel
189      that it was (3.0) hhh. Well I'm frightened
190      that I'm delaying it on pur-y'know-the fear
191      is that (.)I'm delaying it on purpose.
192      (.)
193 T: And if you delay it what might happen?
194      What is this really about? (1.9) If you delay
195      it what would happen?
```

```
196 C: Uhh (.) Well I've failed you see (.)
197 T: Yes. What would failing mean? (.) What would
198    actually happen? I mean in real terms?
199 C: Well I'd give in (.) Well I wouldn't have a
200    relationship.
201 T: Yes. That's right.
202    (.)
203 C: Yes.
204 T: If you don't have one quickly you won't have
205    one at all.
206 C: Haha[ha
207 T:     [hahaha[hahahahahah RIGHT hahaha
208 C:            [Hahahahahahahahahahahhhhhhh not the
209    way you let me plough on! Ha[hahahaha
210 T:                              [HAHAHAHAhaha
211 C: Yes. That's it.
212 T: Yes?
213 C: That's right.
```

APPENDIX 2:3

This extract begins about twenty minutes into a consultation. The therapist has just finished a lengthy turn in which she has been imparting information to the client:

[JP/Ma2/11598]

```
 1 T: Okay. Right. I've been talking a lot again.
 2    .hh um - . Do you think I do talk too
 3    much? >cos when I've looked into some of my
 4    tapes I think there's a lot of me on it.< Is
 5    it help[ful?
 6 C:      [.hhhh Oh I think it is cos it
 7    stimulates ideas in me too=
 8 T: = Good. [That's] what I'm hoping. Yes. [Yes.
 9 C:        [Mmm]                          [And I
10    think that's good as well and it helps me to
11    understand things an[d I] think it probably =
12 T:                     [Yes]
13 C: = reinforces things that I already think
14    anyway [( )] things that I do thin[k but] it =
15 T:       [Mmm]                        [uhum]
16 C: = just sort of y'know brings them to the
17    forefront of my mind and then I think that
```

```
18    probably helps just sort of going over it
19    simp-y'know just sort of what you said about
20    (.) doing things that I find interesting.
21 T: Yes.
22 C: Yeah. And I mean I think that's DEAD RIGHT.
23 T: Mmm (.) mm.
24 C: And u[m (.)] and -and (3.0). Well (.) in =
25 T:      [Mm]
26    = fa-ha[-ct I ] mean - but obviously it's a =
27         [Hh haa]
28 C: = gradual process: one of .hh um - um -
29    probably used (1.0) thinking in terms - of the
30    idea of um(.)conscious competence [and-] =
31 T:                                   [Yes. yes]
32 C: = um - um -unconscious competence and ( )
33    like that (.) um (1.8) and I-I'm certainly
34    in that state where (.) >for example I played
35    cricket yesterday (.) or was it - no -
36    Saturday<[ .hh] um and that was a time =
37 T:         [Mm]
38 C: = when I - was er conscious incom[petence] (.)
39 T:                                   [Haha]
40 C: because I've always thought that - that I
41    love cricket[(.)b]ut I was standing there and =
42 T:            [Yes]
43 C: = it was a lovely day .hh and I was standing
44    there in the field - and I was thinking "WHAT
45    THE BLOODY HELL am I doing HERE[ again" .hh] =
46 T:                                [Heh heh heh]
47 C: = haha it's BOR[ING and I]'m not doing =
48 T:               [hh haha]
49 C: = anyth[ing! I just] stood there =
50 T:       [.hh hahaha ]
51 C: about eight hours and the ball came to me
52    about once! and I was thinking ".hh God!"
53    y'know (1.2) "what am I doing here!" y'know.
54    (0.8) "I just don't like it." and er- so the
55    result is I'm not going to play cricket
56    any more! I'm going to try something
57    different =
58 T: = Oh right. Well that's goo:d - then that
59    just show:s doesn't it that you - you're
60    becoming more and more aware of what you
61    wa:nt and you're realising that lots of
```

```
62     things you've done are the sleepwalking
63     things without really thinking what you want
64     or you don't want. =
65 C:  = but then it's probably because I'm more
66     aware of what I don't want. But then I - I
67     guess that that's part[ of it.
68 T:                    [Right Oh it is.
69     Absolutely. .hh. Oh you've got to know what
70     you don't want. It's like (.) if - if you
71     want to know what good literature is don't
72     only read good literature (.) read bad
73     literature as well
74     (.)
75 C:  No =
76 T:  = because that - I mean that well - y'know
77     inverted commas bad(.)inverted[commas good
78 C:                    [Yeah. Yes[.hh
79 T:                         [Yes.
80     That's fine. It's just exactly what you said
81     in the supermarket. The same thing. You see?
82     (.)
83 C:  Which one's that? Sorry (    )=
84 T:  = the last time on the tape. What you said is
85     almost identical. "What am I doing here?"
86     ((laughing tone)) y'know haha - you don't
87     really want to be there doing the shopping.
88     Right?
89 C:  Right.
90 T:  You grab something and then you go away with
91     the minimum because you make yourself =
92 C:  = Mmm =
93 T:  = But that seems to indicate that you're not
94     too keen on doing shopping.
95     (1.2)
96 C:  (Mm) Mm (2.7) .hhh WE:LL (.) I don't think
97     that means that I (.) don't (.) like shopping
98     deep down- as my actual feeling[ (.) I mean]=
99 T:                      [Ah:: I see ]
100 C: =I think it's different
101    (.)
102 T: Oh (.) Right.
103 C: I think it's more to do with being um (.) led
104    by (.) a sense of ought rather than
105    want[ (.) because] certainly when I was in =
```

106 T: [Oh yes I see]
107 C: = y'know that state a few weeks ago where
108   y'know I was (.) really calm and
109   (.)
110 T: Yes.
111 C: in a state of relaxed concentration and I was
112   was doing what I wanted to do.
113   (.)
114 T: Right
115 C: then it was great and I- shopping was
116   interesting - but y'know - lots of (.)
117   >YE:AH. THAT's a succinct way of putting it<
118   (.) the time when I didn't want to be there =
119 T: Yes
120 C: = because my - my way of thinking (.) was
121   setting myself up for a fall =
122 T: = Yes. Setting yourself up for a fall =
123 C: = whereas - whereas - whereas-when I was (.)
124   there (.) >at this time when I was very calm
125   and relaxed< y'know I could just see
126   that) potential (   ) for more interesting
127   things to happen - y'know - not - plenty of
128   (.) good interesting things to happen -
129   y'know[- if] I'm ( )=
130 T: [Yes]
131 C: = different foods to try y'know - "I might be
132   interested in trying that. I wonder what
133   that's like?" [(.)and (.)] yet - y'know Jean=
134 T: [Yes yes]
135 C: =I mean (2.5)when I get (   ) the - the
136   potential (.) to go from there (.) is massive
137   (.) is enormous - it's unlimited[I think]=
138 T: [Yes yes]
139 C: = be[cause] from then on - because=
140 T: [Yes]
141 C: = I (1.5) in some respects (1.2) y'know my
142   sort of feelings y'know my sort of deep down
143   feelings (.) about what - what I like (.) for
144   example
145   (2.6)
146 T: Mm mm
147 C: massively undeveloped[- and]so it's going=
148 T: [Yes yes]
149 C: = to be(.)like starting from scratch again I

```
150      think but when I've relieved myself of a
151      (.) all these other things in my head which
152      tell me what I ought to be doing etcetera and
153      I can just be calm and relaxed and think what
154      I just want to do =
155 T: = Mm =
156 C: = that will be trial and error as well I think
157      [um but then in] this state =
158 T: [YES indeed mm]
159 C: = that - that's as good as (    ) y'know it's
160      not a problem I sort of think to myself (.)
161      "Okay I don't like it" (.) In the past when I
162      don't like it I kind of think to myself along
163      the lines of "I don't like it and I'll have
164      let myself down" y'know and (.) so many
165      connotations that come up with (.)making a
166      mistake [ and y'know which is ]
167 T:           [Yes yes yes]
168      (2.5)
169 C: I think (.) I think (.) it's quite deeply
170      seated as well (.) but er (    ) yeah -I mean
171      (.) I think =
172 T: = Yes =
173 C: = school's really reinforced it
174      (.)
175 T: Mm
```

APPENDIX 3

References

Alexander, C. (1964). *Notes on the Synthesis of Form.* Cambridge, MA: Harvard University Press.

Antaki, C. & Widdicombe, S. (eds.) (1998). *Identities in Talk.* London: Sage.

Arney, W. & Bergen, B. (1984). *Medicine and the Management of Living.* Chicago University Press.

Atkinson, J.M. & Heritage, J. (eds.) (1984). *Structures of Social Action: Studies in Conversation Analysis.* Cambridge: Cambridge University Press.

Bakhtin, M.M. (1981). *The Dialogic Imagination.* Austin: University of Texas Press.

Bakhtin, M.M. (1986). *Speech Genres and Other Late Essays.* Austin: University of Texas Press.

Bakhtin, M.M. (1994). (edited by Pam Morris) *The Bakhtin Reader.* London: Arnold.

Bancroft, D. & Carr, R. (eds.) (1995). *Influencing Children's Development.* Oxford: Open University, Blackwells.

Bateson, G. (1972). *Steps to an Ecology of Mind: Collected Essays in Anthropology, Psychiatry, Evolution, and Epistemology.* New Jersey: Jason Aaronson Inc.

181

Berne, E. (1966). *Games People Play*. Great Britain: Deutsch. First Published 1964 in U.S.A.

Boden, D. & Zimmerman, D.H. (eds.) (1991). *Talk and Social Structure: Studies in Ethnomethodology and Conversation Analysis*. Cambridge: Polity Press.

Bohart, A.C. & Tallman, K. (1996). The Active Client, Therapy as Self-Help. *Journal of Humanistic Psychology*, 36(3): 7–30.

de Bono, E. (1985). *Conflicts: A Better Way to Resolve Them*. Great Britain: Harrap.

Brown, T.A. (1999). *Genomes*. Oxford: Bios Scientific Publishers.

Cogswell, D. & Gordon, P. (1996). *Chomsky for Beginners*. New York: Writers and Readers Publishing inc.

Cook, V.J. & Newson, M. (1996, second edition). *Chomsky's Universal Grammar*. Oxford: Blackwell.

Drew, P. & Heritage, J. (eds.) (1992). *Talk at Work: Interaction in Institutional Settings*. Cambridge: Cambridge University Press.

Edwards, D. (1998). The Relevant Thing About Her: Social Identity Categories in Use. In Antaki & Widdicombe (1998), pp. 15–33.

Edwards, D. & Potter, J. (eds.) (1992). *Discursive Psychology*. London: Sage.

Farrelly, F. & Brandsma, J. (1974). *Provocative Therapy*. U.S.A. Meta Publications Ltd.

Feltham, C. (2000). Proliferation of Approaches. In Feltham & Horton (2000), pp. 693–5.

Feltham, C. & Horton, I. (eds.) (2000). *Handbook of Counselling and Psychotherapy*. London: Sage.

Ferrara, K.W. (1994). *Therapeutic Ways with Words*. Oxford: Oxford University Press.

Freud, S. (1940). *An Outline of Psychoanalysis*. Volume 23 of the Standard Edition, London: Hogarth Press.

Freud, S. (1957, 1st published 1915e). *The Unconscious*. Volume 14 of the Standard Edition. London: Hogarth Press, pp. 166–204.

Freud, S. (1961, 1st published 1923). *The Ego and the Id*. Volume 21 of the Standard Edition. London: Hogarth Press, pp. 12–68.

Fromm-Reichmann, F. (1960). *Principles of Intensive Psychotherapy*. Chicago: University of Chicago Press. Cited in Sacks (1992).

Garfinkel, H. (1967). *Studies in Ethnomethodology*. Englewood Cliffs: Prentice Hall.

Garfinkel, H. & Sacks, H. (1970). On Formal Structures of Practical Actions. In McKinney & Tiryakian (1970), pp. 337–366.

Goffman, E. (1955). On Face Work. *Psychiatry, 18*: 213–231.

Goffman, E. (1959). *The Presentation of Self in Everyday Life.* London: Penguin.

Goffman, E. (1974). *Frame Analysis.* New York: Harper and Row.

Goffman, E. (1979). Footing. *Semiotica, 25*: 1–29.

Goodwin, C. (1984). Notes on Story Structure and the Organization of Participation. In Atkinson & Heritage (1984), pp. 225–246.

Greenberg, J.H. (ed.) (1963). *Universals of Language.* Cambridge MA: M.I.T. Press, pp. 114–71.

ten Have, P. (1991). Talk and Institution: A Reconsideration of the "Asymmetry" of Doctor/Patient Interaction. In Boden & Zimmerman (1991), pp. 138–163.

Heath, C. (1992). The Delivery and Reception of Diagnosis in the General Practice Consultation. In Drew & Heritage (1992), pp. 235–267.

Heaton, J. & Groves, J. (1994). *Wittgenstein for Beginners.* Cambridge, UK: Icon Books.

Heritage, J. (1984). A Change-of-State Token and Aspects of its Sequential Placement. In Atkinson & Heritage (1984), pp. 299–354.

Heritage, J. & Watson, D.R. (1979). Formulations as Conversational Objects. In Psathas (1979), pp. 123–161.

Holstein, J.A. & Gubrium, J.F. (1997). Qualitative Research: Theory, Method and Practice. In Silverman (1997a), pp. 113–129.

Hutchby, I. (1999). Frame Attunement and Footing in the Organisation of Talk Radio Openings. *Journal of Sociolinguistics 3/1*: 41–63.

Hutchby, I. (2002). Resisting the Incitement to Talk in Child Counselling: Aspects of the Utterance "I don't know". *Discourse Studies, 4(2)*: 147–168.

Hutchby, I. & Moran-Ellis, J. (eds.) (2001). *Children, Technology and Culture: The Impacts of Technologies in Children's Everyday Lives.* London: Routledge/Falmer.

Hutchby, I. & Wooffitt, R. (1998). *Conversation Analysis.* Oxford: Polity Press.

Jefferson, G. (1978). Sequential Aspects of Story-telling in Conversation. In Schenkein (1978), pp. 219–248.

Jefferson, G. (1979). A Technique for Inviting Laughter and its Subsequent Acceptance/Declination. In Psathas (1979), pp. 79–96.

Jefferson, G. (1984). On the Organization of Laughter in Talk about Troubles. In Atkinson & Heritage (1984), pp. 346–369.

Jefferson, G. (1986). On the Interactional Unpacking of a "Gloss". *Language in Society, 14*: 435–66.

Jefferson, G. (1988). On the Sequential Organization of Troubles Talk in Ordinary Conversation. *Social Problems, 35*(4): 418–442.

Jefferson, G. & Lee, J.R.E. (1992). The Rejection of Advice: Managing the Problematic Convergence of "Troubles-Telling" and a "Service Encounter". In Drew & Heritage (1992), pp. 521–548.

Jung, C.G. (1959). *The Archetypes and the Collective Unconscious*. Vol. 9, Part 1 of The Collected Works of C.G. Jung. Princeton: Princeton University Press.

Jung, C.G. (1961). *Memories, Dreams, Reflections*. London: Collins and Routledge & Kegan Paul. Recorded and edited by Aniela Jaffe. Translated from the German by Richard & Clara Winston.

Jung, C.G. (1968, 2nd edition, first published 1959). *The Archetypes and the Collective Unconscious*. Vol. 9, Part 1 of The Collected Works. Princeton: Princeton University Press.

Kahn, M. (2002). *Basic Freud*. U.S.A.: Basic Books.

Korzybski, A. (1933). *Science and Sanity: an Introduction to Non-Aristotelian Systems and General Semantics*. New Jersey: Institute of General Semantics.

Kuhn, T.S. (1962). *The Structure of Scientific Revolutions*. London: University of Chicago Press.

Lakoff, G. (1987). *Women, Fire and Dangerous Things: What Categories Reveal about the Mind*. London: University of Chicago Press.

Levinson, S. (1983). *Pragmatics*. Cambridge: Cambridge University Press.

Lundin, R.W. (1989). *Alfred Adler's Basic Concepts and Implications*. USA: Muncie, AD Accelerated Development Inc.

McGuiness, J. (2000). Therapeutic Climate. In Feltham & Horton (2000), pp. 343–345.

McLeod, J. (2000). Narrative Therapy. In Feltham & Horton (2000), pp. 343–345.

McKinney, J.C. & Tiryakian, E.A. (eds.) (1970). *Theoretical Sociology*. New York: Appleton-Century-Crofts.

Maslow, A. (1954). *Motivation and Personality*. New York: Harper and Row.

Maslow, A. (1962). *Towards a Psychology of Being*. New York: Van Nostrand.

Miell, D. & Dallos, R. (eds.) (1996). *Social Interaction and Personal Relationships*. The Open University. London: Sage.

Opie, P. & Opie, I. (1959). *The Lore and Language of School Children*. Oxford: Clarendon Press.

Pain, J. (2003). *Not Just Talking: A Sociological Study of the Organisation of the Dialogue in One-to-One Psychotherapy*. Brunel University, UK: Unpublished PhD thesis.

Perakyla, A (1995). *Aids Counselling: Institutional Interaction and Clinical Practice*. Cambridge: Cambridge University Press.

Perakyla, A. (1997). Reliability and Validity in Research Based on Transcripts. In Silverman (1997a), pp. 201–220.

Pinker, S. (1995). *The Language Instinct*. London: Penguin.

Pinker, S. (2002). *The Blank Slate*. London: Allen Lane, an imprint of Penguin Books.

Pirsig, R. (1974). *Zen and the Art of Motorcycle Maintenance*. London: Bodley Head.

Pirsig, R. (1991). *Lila: an Enquiry into Morals*. London: Black Swan.

Pomerantz, A. (1984). Agreeing and Disagreeing with Assessments: Some Features of Preferred/Dispreferred Turn Shapes. In Atkinson & Heritage (1984), pp. 57–101.

Pomerantz, A. (1986). Extreme Case Formulations. *Human Studies, 9*: 219–230.

Potter, J. (1997). Discourse Analysis as a Way of Analysing Naturally Occurring Talk. In Silverman (1997a).

Psathas, G. (ed.) (1979). *Everyday Language: Studies in Ethnomethodology*. Hillsdale, N.J. Erlbaum.

Pula, R.P. (1994). Preface to 5th edition of Korzybski's *Science and Sanity*.

Rogers, C.R. (1957). The Necessary and Sufficient Conditions of Therapeutic Personality Change. *Journal of Consulting Psychology, 21*: 95–103.

Rogers, C.R. (1990). *A Therapist's View of Psychotherapy - On Becoming a Person*. London: Constable.

Rosch, E., Mervis, C.B., Gray, W.D., Johnson, D., & Boyes-Braem, P. (1976). Basic Objects in Natural Categories. *Cognitive Psychology, 8*: 382–439

Rose, C. (1985). *Accelerated Learning*. England: Accelerated Learning Systems Ltd.

Russell, B. (1990). *Unpopular Essays* (first pub. 1950). England: Unwin Paperbacks.

Sacks, H. (1984a). On Doing "Being Ordinary". In Atkinson & Heritage (1984), pp. 413–429.

Sacks, H. (1992) .*Lectures on Conversation*. Oxford: Blackwell.

Sacks, H., Schegloff, E.A. & Jefferson, G. (1974). A Simplest Systematics for the Organization of Turn-Taking for Conversation. *Language, 50*: 696–735.

Satir, V. (1967). *Conjoint Family Therapy.* Palo Alto, California: Souvenir Press (E & A Ltd.).

Schegloff, E.A. (1968). Sequencing in Conversational Openings. *American Anthropologist, 70*: 1075–95.

Schegloff, E.A. (1979). The Relevance of Repair to Syntax-for-Conversation. In Givon (1979), pp. 261–288.

Schegloff, E.A. (1982). Discourse as an Interactional Achievement: Some Uses of "uh huh" and Other Things that come between Sentences. In Tannen (1982), pp. 71–93.

Schegloff, E.A. (1984). On Some Questions and Ambiguities in Conversation. In Atkinson & Heritage (1984), pp. 28–52.

Schegloff, E.A. (1987). Analysing Single Episodes of Interaction: an Exercise in Conversation Analysis. *Social Psychology Quarterly, 50*: 101–114.

Schegloff, E.A. (1988). Presequences and Indirection: Applying Speech Act Theory to Ordinary Conversation. *Journal of Pragmatics, 12*: 55–62.

Schegloff, E.A. (1991). Reflections on Talk and Social Structure. In Boden & Zimmerman (1991), 44–70.

Schegloff, E.A. (1992a). Introduction to Sacks' (1992) *Lectures on Conversation. 1*: ix–lxiv.

Schegloff, E.A. (1992b). Introduction to Sacks' Conversation Analysis, 2: ix–l.

Schegloff, E.A. (1992c). On Talk and its Institutional Occasions. In Drew & Heritage, 101–136.

Schegloff, E.A., Jefferson, G., & Sacks, H. (1977). The Preference for Self-correction in the Organization of Repair in Conversation. *Language, 53*: 361–382.

Schegloff, E.A. and Sacks, H. (1973). Opening up Closings. *Semiotica, 7*: 289–327.

Schenkein, J.N. (ed.) (1978). *Studies in the Organisation of Conversational Interaction.* New York: Academic Press.

Siegfried, J. (ed.) (1995). *Therapeutic and Everyday Discourse as Behavior Change: Towards a Micro-Analysis in Psychotherapy Process Research.* New Jersey: Ablex.

Silverman, D. (ed) (1993). *Interpreting Qualitative Data: Methods for Analysing Talk, Text and Interaction*. London: Sage.

Silverman, D. (ed.)(1997a). *Qualitative Research: Theory, Method and Practice*. London: Sage.

Silverman, D. (1997b). *Discourses of Counselling: HIV Counselling as Social Interaction*. London: Sage.

Silverman, D. (1998). *Harvey Sacks: Social Science & Conversation Analysis*. Oxford: Polity Press in association with Blackwells.

Simeons, A.T.W. (1960). *Man's Presumptuous Brain*. New York: Dutton.

Szaz, T. (1962). *The Myth of Mental Illness*. London: Secker & Warburg Ltd.

Torode, B. (ed.) (1989). *Text and Talk as Social Practice*. Dordrecht: Foris.

Velmans, M. (2000). *Understanding Consciousness*. London: Routledge.

Watson, R. (1995). Some Potentialities and Pitfalls in the Analysis of Process and Personal Change in Counselling and Therapeutic Interaction. In Siegfried (1995), pp. 301–340.

Weinreich, U. (1963). On the Semantic Structure of Language. In Greenberg J.H. (ed.) (1963), pp. 114–71.

Wittgenstein, L. (1958). *Philosophical Investigations*. Oxford: Blackwell.

Wood, D. (1995). Teachers' Questions. In Bancroft & Carr (1995), pp. 29–31.

Wowk, M.T. (1989). Emotions in Talk. In Torode (1989), pp. 57–71.

Wowk, M.T. (1995). Mind and Body: Aspects of Personal Change. In Siegfried (1995). pp. 419–446.

Yapko, M. (1989). *Brief Approaches to Treating Anxiety and Depression*. New York: Brunner/Mazel Inc.

INDEX